PLOTINUS
ENNEAD VI.4 and VI.5

THE *ENNEADS* OF PLOTINUS
With Philosophical Commentaries

*Series Editors: John M. Dillon, Trinity College, Dublin
and Andrew Smith, University College, Dublin*

ALSO AVAILABLE IN THE SERIES:

FORTHCOMING TITLES IN THE SERIES INCLUDE:

PLOTINUS
ENNEAD VI.4 and VI.5

On the Presence of Being, One and the Same, Everywhere as a Whole

Translation with an Introduction
and Commentary

EYJÓLFUR K. EMILSSON
and
STEVEN K. STRANGE

PARMENIDES
PUBLISHING

Las Vegas | Zurich | Athens

PARMENIDES PUBLISHING
Las Vegas | Zurich | Athens

This edition published in 2015 by Parmenides Publishing
in the United States of America

ISBN soft cover: 978-1-930972-34-6
ISBN e-Book: 978-1-930972-14-8

Library of Congress Cataloging-in-Publication Data

Plotinus.
    [Ennead. VI. 4-5. English]
  Ennead VI.4 and VI.5 : on the presence of being, one and the same,
everywhere as a whole / PLOTINUS ; translation with an introduction and commentary, EYJÓLFUR K. EMILSSON and STEVEN K.
STRANGE.
        pages cm. -- (The Enneads of Plotinus with philosophical com-
mentaries)
  Includes bibliographical references and index.
  ISBN 978-1-930972-34-6 (pbk. : alk. paper) -- ISBN 978-1-930972-
14-8 (e-book)
1. Soul--Early works to 1800. 2. Plotinus. Ennead. VI. 4-5. I. Eyjólfur Kjalar Emilsson. II. Strange, Steven K. III. Title. IV. Title: On the
presence of being, one and the same, everywhere as a whole.
  B693.E52E5 2014
  186'.4--dc23
                                        2014025565

Typeset in Janson Text & Frutiger by Parmenides Publishing
Printed by Edwards Brothers Malloy, Chicago, IL

www.parmenides.com

Contents

Introduction to the Series
With a Brief Outline of the Life and
Thought of Plotinus (205–270 CE)

PLOTINUS WAS BORN IN 205 CE in Egypt of Greek-speaking parents. He attended the philosophical schools in Alexandria where he would have studied Plato (427–347 BCE), Aristotle (384–322 BCE), the Stoics and Epicureans as well as other Greek philosophical traditions. He began his serious philosophical education, however, relatively late in life, at the age of twenty-seven and was deeply impressed by the Platonist Ammonius Saccas about whom we, unfortunately, know very little, but with whom Plotinus studied for some eleven years. Even our knowledge of Plotinus' life is limited to what we can glean from Porphyry's introduction to his edition of his philosophical treatises, an account colored by Porphyry's own concerns. After completing his studies in Alexandria Plotinus attempted, by joining a military expedition of the Roman emperor Gordian III, to make contact with the Brahmins in order to learn something of Indian thought.

Unfortunately Gordian was defeated and killed (244). Plotinus somehow managed to extract himself and we next hear of him in Rome where he was able to set up a school of philosophy in the house of a high-ranking Roman lady by the name of Gemina. It is, perhaps, surprising that he had no formal contacts with the Platonic Academy in Athens, which was headed at the time by Longinus, but Longinus was familiar with his work, partly at least through Porphyry who had studied in Athens. The fact that it was Rome where Plotinus set up his school may be due to the originality of his philosophical activity and to his patrons. He clearly had some influential contacts, not least with the philhellenic emperor Gallienus (253–268), who may also have encouraged his later failed attempt to set up a civic community based on Platonic principles in a ruined city in Campania.

Plotinus' school was, like most ancient schools of philosophy, relatively small in scale, but did attract distinguished students from abroad and from the Roman upper classes. It included not only philosophers but also politicians and members of the medical profession who wished to lead the philosophical life. His most famous student was Porphyry (233–305) who, as a relative latecomer to the school, persuaded him to put into writing the results of his seminars. It is almost certain that we possess most, if not all, of his written output, which represents his mature thought, since he didn't commence writing until the age of forty-eight. The school seemingly had inner and outer circles, and Plotinus himself was clearly an inspiring and sympathetic teacher who took a deep interest in the philosophical and spiritual progress of his students. Porphyry tells us that when he was suffering from severe depression Plotinus straightaway visited him in his lodgings to help him. His concern for others is also illustrated by the fact that he was entrusted with the personal education of many orphans and the care of their property and careers. The reconciliation of this worldly involvement with the encouragement to lead a life of contemplation is encapsulated in Porphyry's comment that "he was present to himself and others at the same time."

The *Enneads* of Plotinus is the edition of his treatises arranged by his pupil Porphyry who tried to put shape to the collection he had inherited by organizing it into six sets of nine treatises (hence the name *"Enneads"*) that led the reader through the levels of Plotinus' universe, from the physical world to Soul, Intellect and, finally, to the highest principle, the One. Although Plotinus undoubtedly had a clearly structured metaphysical system by the time he began committing himself to expressing his thought in written form, the treatises themselves are not systematic expositions, but rather explorations of particular themes and issues raised in interpreting Plato and other philosophical texts read in the School. In fact, to achieve his neat arrangement Porphyry was sometimes driven even to dividing certain treatises (e.g., III.2–3; IV.3–5, and VI.4–5).

Although Plotinus' writings are not transcripts of his seminars, but are directed to the reader, they do, nevertheless, convey the sort of lively debate that he encouraged in his school. Frequently he takes for granted that a particular set of ideas is already familiar as having been treated in an earlier seminar that may or may not be found in the written text. For this reason it is useful for the reader to have some idea of the main philosophical principles of his system as they can be extracted from the *Enneads* as a whole.

Plotinus regarded himself as a faithful interpreter of Plato whose thought lies at the core of his entire project. But Plato's thought, whilst definitive, does according to Plotinus require careful exposition and clarification, often in the light of other thinkers such as Aristotle and the Stoics. It is because of this creative application of different traditions of ancient thought to the interpretation of Plato that Plotinus' version of Platonism became, partly through the medium of later Platonists such as Porphyry, Iamblichus (245–325), and Proclus (412–485), an influential source and way of reading both Plato and Aristotle in the Middle Ages, the Renaissance, and up to the early 19th century, when scholars first began to differentiate Plato and "Neoplatonism." His thought, too, provided early Christian theologians of the Latin and particularly of the Byzantine tradition, with a rich variety of metaphysical concepts with which to explore and express difficult doctrinal ideas. His fashioning of Plato's ideas into a consistent metaphysical structure, though no longer accepted as a uniquely valid way of approaching Plato, was influential in promoting the notion of metaphysical systems in early modern philosophy. More recently increasing interest has centered on his exploration of the self, levels of consciousness, and his expansion of discourse beyond the levels of normal ontology to the examination of what lies both above and beneath being. His thought continues to challenge us when confronted with the issue of man's nature and role in the universe and of the extent and limitations of human knowledge.

Whilst much of Plotinus' metaphysical structure is recognizably an interpretation of Plato it is an interpretation that is not always immediately obvious just because it is filtered through several centuries of developing Platonic thought, itself already overlaid with important concepts drawn from other schools. It is, nevertheless, useful as a starting point to see how Plotinus attempts to bring coherence to what he believed to be a comprehensive worldview expressed in the Platonic dialogues. The Platonic Forms are central. They become for him an intelligible universe that is the source and model of the physical universe. But aware of Aristotle's criticism of the Platonic Forms as lifeless causes he takes on board

Aristotle's concept of god as a self-thinker to enable him to identify this intelligible universe as a divine Intellect that thinks itself as the Forms or Intelligibles. The doctrine of the Forms as the thoughts of god had already entered Platonism, but not as the rigorously argued identity that Plotinus proposed. Moreover the Intelligibles, since they are identical with Intellect, are themselves actively intellectual; they are intellects. Thus Plato's world of Forms has become a complex and dynamic intelligible universe in which unity and plurality, stability, and activity are reconciled.

Now although the divine Intellect is one it also embraces plurality, both because its thoughts, the Intelligibles, are many and because it may itself be analyzed into thinker and thought. Its unity demands a further principle, which is the cause of its unity. This principle, which is the cause of all unity and being but does not possess unity or being in itself, he calls the One, an interpretation of the Idea of the Good in Plato's *Republic* that is "beyond being" and that may be seen as the simple (hence "one") source of all reality. We thus have the first two of what subsequently became known as the three Hypostases, the One, Intellect, and Soul, the last of which acts as an intermediary between the intelligible and physical universes. This last Hypostasis takes on all the functions of transmitting form and life that may be found in Plato, although Plato himself does not always make such a clear distinction between soul and intellect. Thus the One is the ultimate source of all, including this universe, which is then prefigured in Intellect and transmitted through Soul to become manifest as our physical universe. Matter, which receives imperfectly this expression, is conceived not as an independently existing counter-principle, a dangerously dualist notion, but is in a sense itself a product of the One, a kind of non-being that, while being nothing specific in itself, nevertheless is not simply not there.

But this procession from an ultimate principle is balanced by a return movement at each level of reality that fully constitutes itself only when it turns back in contemplation of its producer. And so the whole of reality is a dynamic movement of procession and return, except for matter, which has no life of its own to make this return; it is inert. This movement of return, which may be traced back to the force of "love" in Plato or Aristotle's final cause, is characterized by Plotinus as a cognitive activity, a form of contemplation, weaker at each successive level, from Intellect through discursive reasoning to the merest image of rational order as expressed in the objects of the physical universe.

The human individual mirrors this structure to which we are all related at each level. For each of us has a body and soul, an intellect, and even something within us that relates to the One. While it is the nature of soul to give life to body, the higher aspect of our soul also has aspirations towards intellect, the true self, and even beyond. This urge to return corresponds to the cosmic movement of return. But the tension between soul's natural duty to body and its origins in the intelligible can be, for the individual, a source of fracture and alienation in which the soul becomes over-involved and overwhelmed by the body and so estranged from its true self. Plotinus encourages us to make the return or ascent, but at the same time attempts to resolve the conflict of duties by reconciling the two-fold nature of soul as life-giving and contemplative.

This is the general framework within which important traditional philosophical issues are encountered, discussed and resolved, but always in a spirit of inquiry and ongoing debate. Issues are frequently encountered in several different contexts, each angle providing a different insight. The nature of the soul and its relationship to the body is examined at length (IV) using the Aristotelian distinctions of levels of soul (vegetative, growth, sensitive, rational) whilst maintaining the immortal nature of the transcendent soul in Platonic terms. The active nature of the soul in sense-perception is maintained to preserve the principle that incorporeals cannot be affected by corporeal reality. A vigorous discussion (VI.4 and 5) on the general nature of the relationship of incorporeals to body explores in every detail and in great depth the way in which incorporeals act on body. A universe that is the product of design is reconciled with the freedom of the individual. And, not least, the time-bound nature of the physical universe and human reason is grounded in the life of Intellect, which subsists in eternity. Sometimes, however, Plotinus seems to break outside the framework of traditional metaphysics: the nature of matter and the One, each as non-being, though in a different sense, strains the terminology and structure of traditional ontology; and the attempt to reconcile the role of the individual soul within the traditional Platonic distinction of transcendent and immanent reality leads to a novel exploration of the nature of the self, the "I."

It is this restless urge for exploration and inquiry that lends to the treatises of Plotinus their philosophical vitality. Whilst presenting us with a rich and complexly coherent system, he constantly engages us in philosophical inquiry. In this way each treatise presents us with new ideas and fresh challenges. And, for Plotinus, every philosophical engagement is not just a mental exercise but also contributes to the rediscovery of the self and our reintegration with the source of all being, the Platonic aim of "becoming like god."

While Plotinus, like Plato, always wishes to engage his audience to reflect for themselves, his treatises are not easy reading, partly no doubt because his own audience was already familiar with many of his basic ideas and, more importantly, had been exposed in his seminars to critical readings of philosophical texts that have not survived to our day. Another problem is that the treatises do not lay out his thought in a systematic way but take up specific issues, although always the whole system may be discerned in the background. Sometimes, too, the exact flow of thought is difficult to follow because of an often condensed mode of expression.

Because we are convinced that Plotinus has something to say to us today, we have launched this series of translations and commentaries as a means of opening up the text to readers with an interest in grappling with the philosophical issues revealed by an encounter with Plotinus' own words and arguments. Each volume will contain a new translation, careful summaries of the arguments and structure of the treatise, and a philosophical commentary that will aim to throw light on the philosophical meaning and import of the text.

John M. Dillon
Andrew Smith

Abbreviations

Armstrong Armstrong, Arthur Hilary. 1966–1982. *Plotinus*. Greek Text with English Translation and Introductions. Cambridge, MA: Loeb.

Bréhier Bréhier, Émile. 1924–1938. *Plotin, Ennéades*. Greek Text and French Translation with Introductions and Notes. Paris: Les Belles Lettres.

Cilento Cilento, Vincenzo. 1947–1949. *Plotino, Enneadi*. Italian Translation and Commentary. Bari: Laterza.

Creuzer Creuzer, Georg Friedrich. 1835. *Plotini Enneades*. Greek Text, with Marsilio Ficino's Latin Translation and Commentary. Oxford: E Typographeo Academico.

HBT Harder, Richard, Rudolf Beutler, and Willy Theiler. 1956–1970. *Plotins Schriften* I–VI. Hamburg: Felix Meiner.

HS₁   Henry, Paul and Hans-Rudolph Schwyzer.
              1951–73. *Plotini Opera* I–III (editio maior).
              Paris: Desclée de Brouwer et Cie.
HS₂   Henry, Paul and Hans-Rudolph Schwyzer.
              1964–1982. *Plotini Opera* I–III (editio
              minor, with revised text). Oxford:
              Clarendon Press.
Kirchhoff Kirchhoff, Adolph. 1856. *Plotini Opera*.
              Leipzig: B. G. Teubner.
LS   Long, Anthony A., and David N. Sedley.
              1987. *The Hellenistic Philosophers, Volume
              1: Translation of the Principal Sources, with
              Philosophical Commentary*. Cambridge:
              Cambridge University Press.
SVF   Von Arnim, Hans, ed. 1905. *Stoicorum
              Veterum Fragmenta*. Leipzig: B. G. Teubner.
Tornau   Tornau, Christian. 1998. *Plotin. Enneaden
              VI 4–5 [22–23]. Ein Kommentar*. Stuttgart
              and Leipzig: B. G. Teubner.

Acknowledgments

THIS TRANSLATION AND COMMENTARY have been in the making since 1990. At that time, during my stay at the Center for Hellenic Studies in Washington D. C., Steven Keith Strange and I decided to translate and comment on *Ennead* VI.4. and 5. And we got to work: Steven quickly produced a draft of a translation of VI.4. and I wrote a draft of an introduction. We discussed the main contentions of the treatise and difficult passages in prolonged conversations. Steven eventually finished a fine draft of a translation of the whole treatise and both of us published articles relating to it. The work on the common project, however, stopped for many years after I left the United States. Both of us soon became preoccupied with other projects and had only very sporadic contact. Each of us, however, felt it was a shame not to finish this.

The necessary stimulus to complete the work came when the editors of the present series contacted me: would I like to contribute? My thoughts immediately went to this old project and I called Steven up. And indeed, he was very much his old self and ready. We spoke for at least half an hour on the phone about this and other things. Shortly afterwards he sent me his latest version of his translation and notes—as opposed to me, he apparently had been working a bit on this over the years. I much looked forward to resuming our collaboration. A few months later the very sad news came that Steven was dead. I still don't know if he was aware of his illness when we spoke on the phone, at least he did not tell me.

So what I had in my hands when I took up this work in 2011 was a good draft of a translation from Steven, some sporadic notes, mostly Steven's, and my old article and thoughts about the treatise. There was nothing like a draft of a commentary. Thus, the commentary presented here is principally my recent work.

In the meantime an excellent, very extensive commentary on the treatise appeared in German: Christian Tornau's *Plotin. Enneaden VI 4–5 [22–23]. Ein Kommentar* from 1998. This work has been a blessing for me in the writing of the present commentary. As readers will see, references to it, overwhelmingly expressing agreement and debt, are numerous. Undoubtedly, the debts cut deeper than what is explicitly acknowledged. Certain modifications of Steven's translation turned out to be necessary in light of Tornau's arguments concerning particular passages and some for other reasons. Where changes have been made, I have sought to keep Steven's style.

Thanks are due to several people who have assisted with advice and comments: Christian Tornau, Dominic J. O'Meara, and the general editors of the series, Andrew Smith and John Dillon. I wish to thank especially my assistants, Lars Gjøvikli and Panagiotis Pavlos, for a meticulous job in the final phase of the work, and my department, the Department of Philosophy, Classics, History of Art and Ideas at the University of Oslo, for making it possible for me to have an assistant for an extended period.

Introduction to the Treatise

1. General remarks

The treatises VI.4–5 are number 22 and 23 on Porphyry's chronological list of Plotinus' treatises. They constitute the first work of Plotinus' middle period of writing, which spans over the six years Porphyry stayed with him in Rome and during which Plotinus wrote twenty-four treatises. Here the counting is according to Porphyry's splitting-up of treatises, which he did in order to reach the total number of 54 (see *Life of Plotinus* 24). Our treatise thus precedes, but not by much, the long treatise IV.3–5 "On the problems of soul" (split into three by Porphyry and numbered 27–29 in the chronological list). According to this, a likely year of composition is 262. Our treatise, VI.4–5, originally a single, continuous work, is another case of one that got split-up. Both in what follows here and in the commentary we speak of it as a single treatise, as it was in fact conceived by its author.

Porphyry provided the traditional titles of Plotinus' treatises. In this case, he borrowed the title from Plato's

Parmenides 131b1–2 and 144c8–d1: "On Being, Being One and the Same, Being Everywhere at Once as a Whole," or as we might also say, slightly less inelegantly, "On the Presence of Being, One and the Same, Everywhere as a Whole." As we shall see, in a way this title does indeed describe the content of the treatise fairly accurately. It is, however, misleading in that it does not mention soul, whereas for the most part the being which is said to be everywhere at once as a whole in the treatise is soul, and not what the title and its Parmenidean origin may suggest, namely the Platonic Ideas. This latter topic is indeed addressed but the main focus is on the soul-body relationship.

Our treatise deals with deep philosophical topics. It addresses and in a way coalesces two central issues in Platonism, namely the nature of the soul-body relationship and the nature of participation. It contains Plotinus' most general and sustained exposition of the relationship between the intelligible and sensible realms. The treatise seems to have had considerable impact: it is much reflected in Porphyry's important work, *Launching points leading to the intelligibles* (or *Sententiae*, as it is often called) and, as we shall see below, the doctrine of reception according to the capacity of the recipient, for which our treatise is the main source, resonated in medieval thinkers.

2. The main thesis: the intelligible is undivided and bodies participate in it as a whole

Plotinus begins the treatise by raising the following questions:

> Is the reason that soul is everywhere present to the universe that the body of the universe has a certain size, and it is the nature of soul to be "divisible about bodies"? Or is soul everywhere just in virtue of itself, so that it is not just located wherever body may happen to have brought it, but instead body finds soul to be everywhere prior to it, so that wherever it is put, it finds that soul was already there before it was placed in that part of the universe, and so that the whole body of the universe is placed in an already existing soul?

Both of these initial questions, which are based on interpretations of Plato's *Timaeus* 35a and 36e, respecttively, presuppose that the soul animating the sensible universe is extended and hence divisible. The difference is only whether the soul is thought to be present in any extension prior to body or becomes extended as a result of ensouling the body in all its parts. In either case it is extended and, hence, divisible: spatial extension for

Plotinus implies divisibility (*merismos*), which in the context of our treatise means to be divisible into different spatial parts. If the soul really is divisible, its overarching, superior nature with respect to the body and, in fact, its membership in the intelligible realm becomes suspect. For it is precisely in virtue of possessing a higher degree of unity that the intelligible is distinguished from the sensible. The matter is even worse if the soul should become divisible as a result of its communion with the body, for that would mean that the soul, which is supposed to be the cause of the sensible realm, is affected by its own effect; that would constitute a violation of one of Plotinus' fundamental principles: the ontologically prior is not affected by the posterior. So we have a dilemma here.

We get the gist of Plotinus' solution to this problem in the three subsequent chapters. The rest is further attempts at elucidating this solution, defences of it against objections and rejections of alternatives. In addition, there are some excursions into side issues. As we shall see, Plotinus' solution is highly abstract. It addresses the intelligible-sensible relation quite generally. It goes together with this that distinctions he elsewhere emphasizes and even focuses on are either ignored or left in the background. For instance, the distinctions between the hypostasis Soul, Intellect, and the One do not play any significant role here. Likewise, the distinctions between kinds of soul and soul activities—e.g., World-Soul, individual human souls, perceptive soul, nutritive soul that Plotinus is careful to make for instance in the chronologically close treatise, "The problems of soul"—are of no great importance. In our treatise he is primarily concerned with a categorical distinction between ontological realms and he brushes details aside.

In order to see Plotinus' solution in context, it is worthwhile to have an overview over the relevant parts of his world.

The sensible sphere consists of matter, bodies, and forms in matter. Bodies are characterized by divisibility (4.8, 18–19; IV.2.2). This means that they are spatially extended and no part of a body is the same as any other, each of the infinitely many parts is a unique individual entity. Forms in matter or qualities are specifically the same in many—the white in this sheet and the white in that one are the same in form (*eidei*). Nevertheless, forms in matter belong to their bodies and are individuated by them. It follows that these forms are divisible along with their bodies (4.1, 17–28; IV.2.1). They count as members of the sensible realm rather than the intelligible. Matter as such is not a topic in our treatise, even though matter's participation in Ideas is discussed in 5.8. Nor is the generation of matter by soul discussed, and the generation of bodies is only a side issue discussed in 5.8–9 and cursorily treated in 5.6 and 5.11. Plotinus' general doctrine is that matter, body, and qualities are produced by the World-Soul.[1] We do not see clear evidence of this here: the only passage that fully addresses the generation of bodies is, as already mentioned, 5.8, which only speaks of the participation of matter in Ideas without any mention of the mediation of soul (see Commentary 5.8).

Let us then turn to the intelligible realm. First a note on terminology: the term "the intelligible" (*to noēton*) is used here and often in the Commentary as a collective term for any kind of soul, Intellect, (real) being, substance (*ousia*) and Platonic Ideas, and may even include the One. This is in accordance with one of the uses of *to noēton* in Plotinus. Even if "the intelligible" is not as prominent a term in our treatise as in some others, it comes in handy as a collective contrastive term to the sensible and corporeal. It is a well-known Plotinian claim that Intellect (*nous*), being (*on*), substance (*ousia*), and Ideas (*ideai, eidē*) are identical or at least coextensive.[2] He also frequently claims that the soul is an intelligible thing (see, e.g., IV.1.1, 1–3; IV.2.1, 5ff.; IV.4.2, 13ff.) and indeed a substance (see, e.g., II.3.15, 22; IV.7.5⁵, 49–50; IV.9.4, 26–27).

---

1   On the generation of matter see O'Brien (1991) and (1996).

2   We adopt here the convention of translating *on* and *onta* by "being" and "beings" whereas *ousia* is rendered as "substance." The boundaries between these terms are, however, unclear. Often they seem to denote the same thing, i.e., self-subsisting being. See further Corrigan (1996).

The intelligible rests in itself, it is whole, indivisible and infinite (unlimited, *apeiros*). It follows that it has no place, and in general the logic of parts and wholes that applies to bodies does not apply to it. This means that even if the intelligible is variegated, i.e. contains different beings, each of these beings carries the whole with it: each is not this part at the exclusion of everything else like in the case of bodies. It follows also that it is outside time, because time involves unfolding and dividing what originally and in itself is undivided (5.11, 14–38). From the infinity of the intelligible follows that it is in no way limited by corporeal quantity: make the body to be animated as large as you like, the intelligible will never be exhausted. These are the main points about the nature of the intelligible. Most of them appear already in Chapters 4.2, 4.3 and 4.4.

The theme of the intelligible being at once one and whole, and at the same time variegated, is touched upon a number of times in our treatise (especially in 4.4; 4.14; 5.5; 5.6). Plotinus does not, however, present a prolonged and systematic account of what this means and why this is so in our treatise. This claim about unity-in-multiplicity frequently occurs together with the phrase "all together," *homou pan* or *homou panta*, which he has from Parmenides or Anaxagoras, or both. He applies it to the intelligibles primarily to convey the meaning that they are not spatially or temporally separated: since they are not located anywhere in physical space and not subject to time, they must be all together. The holism about the intelligibles in which Plotinus believes cuts deeper, however, than a mere negation of spatiality and temporality: the intelligibles make up a kind of organic whole. This means that each intelligible is not just itself in isolation but carries with it internal references to the whole to which it belongs and to the other items in that whole. In the treatise "On the intelligible beauty" he says for instance:

> For all things there [in the intelligible world] are transparent, and there is nothing dark or opaque; everything and all things are clear to the inmost part to everything; for light is transparent to light. Each there has everything in itself and sees all things in every other, so that all are everywhere and each and every one is all and the glory is unbounded.... the sun there is all the stars, and each star is the sun and all the others. A different kind of being stands out in each, but in each all are manifest. (V.8.4, 4–11)

What he presumably means is not that the sun is the same thing as, e.g., Venus, but that an account of what the sun is will involve an account of Venus and the other heavenly bodies. This is indeed the point of the comparisons with the sciences that he frequently makes in order to describe this unity-in-multiplicity (cf. 4.4, 44–45; 4.16, 32–36). A proper science has the relevant kind of organic unity: each part, e.g., a particular theorem, receives its identity from the axioms and definitions of the science.

This holism has further consequences. Even if the strictly sensible sphere is an image of the intelligible one, it is an image that has lost the ties that connect it with the whole: a stone is just a stone, nothing more to it. In so far as the sensible sphere is ensouled, however, it carries with it a connection to the whole of being. Or to put this more in accordance with the strict message of our treatise: in virtue of the undivided soul in which the sensible world participates, as a whole and in part, this sensible sphere can be seen as an organic whole itself in which the different parts are not disconnected but in sympathetic relations to one another.

Given this presentation of the sensible and the intelligible, we are in a position to present Plotinus' solution to the initial puzzles. This solution involves turning around and redefining some familiar relations: the body is in soul rather than soul in body, the notion of "being in" is redefined as meaning "depending on," and the claim that being is everywhere is interpreted as meaning that being is in being, i.e., in itself.[3] The intelligible, including soul, does not come to body and is never in the body as in a place. It is body that comes to or reaches out to or participates in the intelligible. That "coming" or "reaching out to" is not a physical coming or outreach to a place, nor is the "participation" a physical sharing. The result of the coming, outreach, or participation—Plotinus seems to use these expressions in more or less the same sense—is that body comes to be in soul. Since the intelligible is "in itself" and is non-spatial, to be "in" the intelligible is not to be in any particular place. That body is in being (soul, the intelligible), which is everywhere, means that the ensouled body will in all its parts depend on the intelligible. But, as already noted, the intelligible is indivisible. It follows that when the body so depends on it, it depends on it as a whole. When the body comes to be in the intelligible, the intelligible is present to it and the body receives of it. Since the intelligible is indivisible, if some of it is present to a body, all of it is. Or vice versa—the relation of presence is reciprocal—if a body is present to the intelligible, it is present to the whole of it.

3. Corollary: Reception according to the capacity of the recipient

Plotinus' solution involves a problem: if the intelligi-

---

3   For further elucidation of these redefinitions see O'Meara (1980).

ble is indivisible and always comes as a whole, should not everything participate in it equally and, hence, be alike? But not everything is alike. How are we to explain the apparent differences among animated bodies? The answer given to this problem is the doctrine of reception according to the capacity (*dynamis*) or the particular adaptability (*epitēdeiotēs*) of the recipient.[4] That is to say, some bodies will only receive and activate this, others that; and some will only receive so much, others less. This, however, has nothing to do with what is present to them—the intelligible, being non-spatial, non-temporal, and indivisible is present as a whole. What of the intelligible becomes activated depends on the capacity of the body to receive and activate.

The doctrine of reception according to capacity of the recipient appeals to differences among recipients to explain differences in the outcome of participation. The question then naturally arises how the differences among recipients are to be explained. Obviously Plotinus cannot endlessly appeal to this doctrine to account for differences: either he must hold that there are different, ultimate recipients or that, at some point, there are some differences in the input from the intelligible. We know that he does not accept the first alternative, which in any case would simply leave the differences in the ultimate

---

4   See Lee (1979) and O'Meara (1980).

recipient as an unexplained basic fact. In his system the ultimate recipient is prime matter, which is without any qualities and apparently without any differentiation. So differences in matter cannot explain why some matter becomes fire, other earth, yet other water or air. It appears that Plotinus was aware of considerations such as these (cf. especially 5.11, 34ff.), but he does not address them in full depth. It seems that he is committed to holding that at least the original differentiation of bodies is to be explained somehow by appeal to differences in the intelligible input. If this is so, the doctrine of reception according to the capacity of the recipient is not a universal principle, but of limited application.

Plotinus is the author of the phrase "reception according to the capacity of the recipient," and he was the first to formulate such a doctrine. The phrase, and at least the basic idea of the doctrine, must be described as something of a hit: it was picked up by the subsequent late ancient and, especially, the medieval tradition, both Islamic and Christian. There are echoes of it in Porphyry's *Sententiae* (29, 21–22; 38, 11) and it found its way into the *Liber de causis*, and from there into medieval thinkers such as Albertus Magnus, Thomas Aquinas and many others.[5]

5　On Aquinas' use of this principle, see Tomarchio (1999). Tomarchio notes that while Aquinas attributes it to Pseudo-Dionysios it cannot be found in his writings, at least not explicitly

4. The course of the treatise

The main thesis of the treatise has already been indicated by the middle of the second chapter, along with Plotinus' fundamental reasons for endorsing it. Chapters 4.3 and 4.4 add a few important points: 4.3 about reception according to the capacity of the recipient and 4.4 about the unity-in-multiplicity of the intelligible itself. The rest of the treatise is occupied with clarifying and articulating the central claim about the undivided presence of the intelligible, refuting alternatives to it (e.g., 4.3, 1–19; 4, 9–10), responding to possible objections that might be raised against it (4.4, 7–18; 4.9–10), attempting to argue for it from common conceptions (5.1–2), and to demonstrate it directly from proper first principles (5.3). Last but not least he tries to make the thesis seem plausible, or at least less implausible, by invoking analogies from something familiar (4.7; 4.12; 5.5), for Plotinus is aware that it has certain extremely paradoxical features and consequences (cf. 4.4, 4–6).

There are some excursions into what can be regarded as side issues. For instance, 4.6 contains an interesting but

formulated. *Liber de causis* (*Book on causes*) is a tractate attributed to Aristotle that circulated first in the Islamic world in Arabic (9th century) and later in a Latin translation (12th century). It turns out, however, that the work is an excerpt from the *Elements of Theology* of Proclus and Plotinian texts. On *Liber de causis* see Cristina D'Ancona Costa (1995) and Richard C. Taylor (1998).

cryptic discussion about sense-perception and the unity of consciousness. The occasion is the question why my soul is limited to my body, a question that arises naturally from the fact that the intelligible, including soul, is whole and undivided. Chapter 4.10 contains a very interesting elucidation of Plotinus' understanding of the paradigm-likeness relation. Again, this is connected to the main theme: if the transcendent intelligible has the role of paradigm and the immanent soul the role of a likeness, it cannot be the case that the a likeness is cut off from its paradigm: the case of a true likeness is different from that of the portrait which can stay on independently of its maker and its model. In the last three chapters of VI.4 Plotinus turns to eschatological questions about the different fates of individual souls after death. As in the previous cases, these considerations are prompted by the main theme: the universality of soul raises the question of how some souls can be good and others evil; if they are all one, we should perhaps think they are all equally good or bad. In VI.5 there are several places that direct the attention to our individual place and role in the ontological structure that for the most part has been described in quite objective and general terms. Thus, in 5.7 he brings up our individual relation to the intelligible, and the last chapter, 5.12, is an eloquent description of the non-discursive experience of being one with the whole intelligible universe. Perhaps this ending suggests that the objective,

impersonal accounts that occupy most of the treatise ultimately serve an ethical end.

There are indications in the text of the treatise that
Plotinus sees himself as changing the topic. This does not
mean that everything falling under a given topic, so conceived, is fully unitary: he may start from a certain question the discussion of which will lead into something fairly
remote. It may, however, be useful to note these divisions,
which are marked by a new question or other clear signs of
a shift. The division here follows Tornau (10–11):

> 4.1–3   Initial question, solution and
> follow-up: What is the relation between
> soul and extension? In what sense is the
> soul said to be everywhere in that which
> it ensouls? Body is in an indivisible soul
> (being) and receives of it according to its
> capacity.
>
> 4.4–6   New question concerning the
> plurality of beings and souls; undimin-
> ished giving; the unity of souls and indi-
> vidual experiences.
>
> 4.7–10 Discussion closed at the end of
> 4.6. Analogies from the sensible sphere;
> rejection of powers that are cut off from
> their sources.

4.11–13 Discussion closed at the end of 4.10; new question at 4.11, 1. If the intelligible is undividedly present to many, how are differences between the many to be explained? The analogy of a voice; the nature of participation.

4.14–16 New question at 4.14, 1. The individual soul considered from an ethical and eschatological standpoint.

5.1–3 Break and resumption of the main topic announced at the end of 4.16. The common conception of one and the same god in us all; the main thesis considered in light of principles proper to the intelligibles.

5.4–7 New argument announced at 5.4, 1. The one god is present to everything; the analogy of a circle and its center; each ensouled being receives the whole but only a part is activated.

5.8–10 Announcement of a new theme at 5.8, 1. The participation of matter in Ideas; the whole cosmos is animated by one life; the individual soul's relation to the Good and the intelligible realm.

5.11   New question at 5.11, 1. The
soul reaches over a great expanse without
being divided; the intelligible is outside
time.

5.12   New question at 5.12, 1. The
human soul can grasp the whole intelligible realm and itself as an integral part of
it by abandoning non-being.

Philosophically speaking our treatise must count
among Plotinus' most penetrating ones. It is a sustained
attempt at coming to grips with the intelligible-sensible
relation, a very difficult and demanding topic for any
Platonist. Even if earlier works contain hints in the
direction of what we get in our treatise, we see these
hints here brought to fruition and considered from many
different angles. Moreover, its central claim about the
undivided presence of the intelligible has consequences for
other central aspects of Plotinus' thought—in particular his
doctrine of double activity and the accompanying notions
of powers and emanation. This will be addressed below.

It must be said, however, that our treatise does not
constitute a particularly accomplished piece of writing.
There is hardly any detectable strategy of organization.
Even if the very last chapter shows some of Plotinus' lit-
erary skills and can be said to be an elegant finale, the

treatise as a whole lacks crescendo. Plotinus admits that his central claim about the undivided presence of the intelligible is paradoxical. He resumes it repeatedly in the course of the treatise in an attempt to make it more palatable. Some of the ideas he comes up with in doing so, e.g., the comparisons with familiar phenomena that he claims illustrate his point in 4.7 and 4.12, are quite interesting. The same can be said of his use of the "common notion" of one and the same god in each of us in 5.1ff. Also of interest is the point he insists on in 5.2 that it is sense-perception, which is suited for corporeal nature, and discursive reason, which is adapted to sense-perception, that make us disbelieve his thesis. It would have been interesting to see these claims more developed. Refutations of alternatives, such as we see in 5.9, contribute to clarifying Plotinus' position and the motivation behind it. Nevertheless, there is not much substantially new, as far as the main thesis is concerned, after the few first chapters. Indeed, the treatise can give the impression of being repetitive. In fairness, however, on close reading the repetitions tend to bring in some new context and show the main thesis in a slightly new light. So perhaps Plotinus can be said to have made his main thesis clearer and more believable by the end of the treatise.

5. The treatise VI.4–5 in the context of Plotinus' writings

In earlier and indeed also in later treatises, Plotinus often speaks as if soul somehow descends into body and animates it—a kind of language he for the most part avoids here. He insists throughout his writings, however, that the soul that comes to be present in a body is an independent substance and of a quite different nature than bodies. The different nature and status of the soul is shown, for instance, by the fact that the soul is present as a whole to the different parts of the body it animates. We see this claim in our treatise in 4.1, 25–26 (cf. the earlier IV.7.6–7 and IV.2.2, and the later IV.4.19, 12–15).

Plotinus never discards this view. In our treatise, however, there are signs indicating that he does not simply think that the soul is a very peculiar thing that manages to be in many places at once gives quite the right picture. Thus, he seeks to use a different language with new metaphors to describe the situation: it is not so much that the soul comes to be in the different parts of the body in the ordinary sense of being *in* something; rather the body as a whole comes to be in the soul. The soul, however, is not divisible, nor is it something localizable; hence, if the body is going be in it, it will be in it as a whole and not as something to be found at some particular place. Admittedly, he speaks of the body as "approaching soul"—an expression that originally signified a movement in space. But clearly, this is not to be taken literally: it is meant as another term for what Platonists call participation.

This way of describing the matter calls for other revisions. One of the backbones of Plotinus' philosophy is his doctrine of double activity that characterizes every stage of his hierarchy from the One downwards, except the very bottom. Allusions to double activity are to be found all over the *Enneads* but it is rarely an issue in its own right.[6] We can say that the doctrine of double activity is basically the story of the "dynamics" of the making of everything from the One. Each level in the hierarchy from the One on is characterized by a definite kind of internal activity that defines the given level. At the same time, this internal activity produces an effect outside itself. This effect is its external activity. The external activity converts toward its source, and is thereby filled with information from it. This constitutes the new level with its own internal activity, which in turn produces an external act. This cycle is repeated till the purely sensible level is reached, where matter, bodies, and bodily forms are the last external acts of soul.

Emanation metaphors are integral to this doctrine of double activity: the external act is typically described as some kind of "out-going" (*proodos*) from the source,

---

6   The fullest account is to be found in V.4.2, 21–37. On double activity, see Emilsson (2007, ch. 1) with further references.

likened to the heat or light from a fire or other such emanations. The external act is also described as a "power" (*dynamis*) of the source, the internal activity. Furthermore, the internal and the external acts are described in the Platonic language of paradigm and image, the external act, being weaker and more dispersed, of course having the role of the image.

All this is of some importance for the understanding of our treatise. At first sight we might think that our treatise goes against the whole idea of double activity and emanation. Not only are the typical emanation metaphors absent, Plotinus even seems to distance himself from the language of powers and of illumination (4.3, 1ff.; 5.8, 10ff.). A closer inspection, however, reveals that this is not quite so. What is of crucial importance in our treatise, a point insisted on a number of times, is that the soul or whatever intelligible comes to be present to sensibles is *not cut off* (*ouk apotetmēmenon*) from its source (e.g., 4.3, 9; 4.9, 15; 5.1, 8). This notion of "not being cut off from" is an essential feature of the double act doctrine, strongly emphasized in the most representative passages for the doctrine.[7] Plotinus' main concern in our treatise is that the soul, despite its dealings with and presence to the sensible, does not lose its ties to the intelligible

---

7   The expression and the idea behind it stems from Aristotle, who in *Physics* 3.3.202b7–8 describes transitive activity such as teaching as the activity of X in Y. See Lloyd (1986, 167ff.) and (1989, 99–100).

as a whole, that it, in fact, always carries with it that whole. Plotinus' skepticism toward powers here is only directed at a conception of powers according to which the powers become detached from their sources. His correction of his own usual talk about "illumination" is also limited in scope: it only relates to the spatial aspects of the metaphor: we should not think of Platonic Ideas as something placed on high, casting light down on matter.

Still the question may be raised as to whether the absence of emanation metaphors and of clear references to internal and external acts indicates that the doctrine of our treatise is a "non-standard" Plotinus.[8] We do not think so. We must bear in mind that Plotinus' main concern is the integrity of soul and that he is only minimally concerned with the distinction between soul, on the one hand, and Intellect and being, on the other. So he is not concerned about accounting for soul as the external act of Intellect or about the embodied soul as an external act of the transcendent soul. This does not mean that he would deny such an account or sees himself as saying anything incompatible with it. It is simply not what he is interested in here. It remains true that it would have been highly interesting to see Plotinus address in full the implications of his claims in our treatise for other tenets of his philosophy, including the double act doctrine. But, alas, we do not get this.

---

8   Thus, Lee (1979, 82–83) holds that the line of argument in VI.4–5 rejects emanationism. That is surely going too far.

6. The soul-body relation and participation

As we have seen, the question Plotinus proposes to discuss at the outset of our treatise, and which introduces the main topic, concerns the nature of the soul and the soul-body relation: is it due to the soul itself or to the nature of the body of the whole that the soul is present everywhere in the whole? However, it turns out that a large part of his answer to this question is about being (the intelligible, the true whole) and the nature of the sensible's participation in being quite generally. The latter has commonly been taken as the main theme of the treatise, the issue about the soul being understood as a mere introduction to the more fundamental problem about the relationship between the sensible and intelligible being.[9]

It is our view, however, that even if Plotinus indeed addresses the question about the relationship between being and sensibles in quite general terms in the subsequent chapters of the treatise, he does not abandon the topic of the relationship between soul and body.[10] He does not think he has changed the subject. The reason is fairly simple: the soul is a full member of the intelligible realm. The soul is, however, the phase of this realm that is most closely related to the sensible; hence, the most pressing questions about the exact relationship

---

9   Cf. Hugo von Kleist (1881), Bréhier, Émile (1936, 161ff.), and Lee (1979).

10   See Emilsson (1993) and (1994).

between the intelligible (being) and the sensible arise concerning the relationship between the soul, considered as a particular case of the intelligible, and the sensible. Indeed, the soul is the only intelligible item that it might be tempting to describe as divisible and otherwise subject to the vicissitudes of bodies. Thus, we might say that the soul is the difficult case. In order to deal adequately with the problem of soul, Plotinus finds it necessary to address the nature of the intelligible and its relation to the sensible quite generally. Clearly, however, it is the case of the soul that occupies his mind throughout most of the treatise and this explains why he shifts from talking about soul to talking about being and vice versa. We see examples of such a shift at the end of 4.1, where he announces a fresh attack on the question about soul and then proceeds to discuss "the true whole" and being in 4.2. Again, at 4.3, 1–4 and 20; 4.6, 1–4; and 4.12, 21, the explicit occurrence of the word "soul" shows that this is what he has in mind in the surrounding discussions too, which seem to be focused on being and the intelligible generally.

This interpretation is neatly confirmed if we consider Plotinus' treatment of the two Platonic passages that more than any others lurk in the background of our treatise. There is the Sailcloth Dilemma from *Parmenides* 131b3–c8: how can one and the same Form be as a whole in things that are many and separate? And there is the celebrated passage in the *Timaeus* 35a about the constitution of the soul, where Plato describes the soul as a mixture of the Same, the Different, and Being, and says that it is intermediate between that which is changeless and partless and that which comes to be in the corporeal realm. The *Parmenides* passage sets the agenda for the bulk of our treatise, whereas Plotinus' solution is, if not what we nowadays would recognize as an interpretation of the *Timaeus* passage, then at least his explication of its meaning: the soul's ontological status is such that it is not divided about bodies.

To state this succinctly: Plato's *Parmenides* may suggest that the problem of participation is a problem about explaining sensible items'—e.g., several large mountains'—participation in a Form, largeness, for example. The question would be whether each of the particular mountains has a share in a part of the Form or whether they somehow all have a share in all of it. If the former, the Form is divisible. If the latter, how is that to be explained? How can the same thing be in many different ones? While Plotinus clearly thinks that the sensible objects participate in the Idea as a whole, the problem of explaining this is not what preoccupies him in our treatise. As noted, he addresses the participation of prime matter in Ideas in 5.8, and he very briefly discusses the issue of many human beings vs. one Idea of Man in 5.6. In 4.1 he admits that corporeal qualities are indeed "the same in form" even if they are in different locations. And he insists that the Idea itself is not split up in participation of this sort. He does not seem to regard the sameness in form in many particulars as a challenging problem, however, because, as noted above, he thinks these qualities have become different individuals. He does see the problem raised in *Parmenides* 131b3–c8 as a serious one, however. But it is a problem about soul: what may seem to be the case is that soul is just like "white"—different in every bodily instance. Yet Plotinus is convinced that this is not the case; hence, his concern to keep the unity of the soul unaffected by its apparent embodiment. This in turn means that Plotinus connects the answer to the riddle posed by the *Parmenides* to the interpretation of *Timaeus* 35a: the latter passage is to be interpreted in such a way that the integrity of soul is preserved; that same concern directs his attitude towards the former.

Another aspect of the integrity of soul is the thesis of the unity of all souls. This is an idea Plotinus presents in his early, rather short, treatise, IV.9, and seems to hold on to. It is evident in many places in our treatise. He plays with the idea that all souls in the world are but one soul in the same way as that in which the body of an organism is animated by one and the same soul in its different parts (cf. 4.6). Our treatise gives the theoretical underpinnings for this doctrine: whatever body participates in soul so as to become ensouled participates in the whole of soul, in fact in the whole of being. Given this thesis of our treatise, it is indeed difficult to see how all soul could fail to be just one soul. In this way one can see the motivation for this paradoxical claim about souls from the basic contention, equally paradoxical, of our treatise: the identity of all souls simply follows from the unity and wholeness of being. This is not all, however: despite the substantial identity of souls, Plotinus also wishes to hold that there are differentiations between souls, both at the intelligible and the sensible level. It must be said that his attempt at reconciling these differentiations with the claim of identity remains obscure (see Commentary on 4.6).

But even if the soul is a being, it is not to be equated with the realm of being in general, which also includes the transcendent Intellect. Intellect is being as such, whereas the soul is being in relation to the sensible world, concerned with informing it and animating it. Once we realize that the soul belongs to the realm of being, and in particular that it is being as it relates to the sensible world, we can see that the sensible's participation in being is for Plotinus the informing and animation of the sensible by the soul: participation and informing/

animation are the same process seen from different perspectives. What from the soul's point of view is the process of informing and animating of the sensible world is from the point of view of the sensible participation in being. The indivisibility of being implies that whatever participates in being participates in being as a whole. From this it follows that the thesis of the indivisibility of the soul is the same thesis as that of participation in being as a whole.

Note on the Text

LINE NUMBERS IN THE TRANSLATION are approximate and do not always match the original Greek text. Since the commentary follows the sequence of the English translation, there may sometimes be a slight discrepancy in the ordering.

The Greek text adopted is that of the Oxford edition (taking into account the *Addenda ad Textum* in vol. 3, 304–325). Deviations from the text are noted in the commentary. Each *Ennead* is referred to by Roman numerals, followed by the number of the treatise, the chapter of the treatise, and, finally, separated by a comma, the line number or numbers, e.g., V.1.3, 24–27.

It is customary to add the chronological number given by Porphyry in his *Life of Plotinus (Vita Plotini)*, so that, for example, V.1 is designated V.1 [10]. In this series the chronological number is given only where it is of significance for Plotinus' philosophical stance. The following charts indicate the chronological order.

It should be noted that Plotinus did not provide titles to the treatises and that these were later added by

Porphyry when preparing his edition from those that had become traditional amongst the readers of Plotinus' manuscripts (see Porphyry *VP* 4), although Porphyry himself sometimes gives different titles to the same treatise in his chronological *VP* 4–6) and thematic (*VP* 24–25) lists, and variant titles are also found in Simplicius and Philoponus in the 6th century.

Chronological Order of the *Enneads*

Enn.		Enn.		Enn.		Enn.		Enn.		Enn.	
I.1	53	II.1	40	III.1	3	IV.1	21	V.1	10	VI.1	42
I.2	19	II.2	14	III.2	47	IV.2	4	V.2	11	VI.2	43
I.3	20	II.3	52	III.3	48	IV.3	27	V.3	49	VI.3	44
I.4	46	II.4	12	III.4	15	IV.4	28	V.4	7	VI.4	22
I.5	36	II.5	25	III.5	50	IV.5	29	V.5	32	VI.5	23
I.6	1	II.6	17	III.6	26	IV.6	41	V.6	24	VI.6	34
I.7	54	II.7	37	III.7	45	IV.7	2	V.7	18	VI.7	38
I.8	51	II.8	35	III.8	30	IV.8	6	V.8	31	VI.8	39
I.9	16	II.9	33	III.9	13	IV.9	8	V.9	5	VI.9	9

	Enn.		Enn.		Enn.		Enn.		Enn.		Enn.
1	I.6	10	V.1	19	I.2	28	IV.4	37	II.7	46	I.4
2	IV.7	11	V.2	20	I.3	29	IV.5	38	VI.7	47	III.2
3	III.1	12	II.4	21	IV.1	30	III.8	39	VI.8	48	III.3
4	IV.2	13	III.9	22	VI.4	31	V.8	40	II.1	49	V.3
5	V.9	14	II.2	23	VI.5	32	V.5	41	IV.6	50	III.5
6	IV.8	15	III.4	24	V.6	33	II.9	42	VI.1	51	I.8
7	V.4	16	I.9	25	II.5	34	VI.6	43	VI.2	52	II.3
8	IV.9	17	II.6	26	III.6	35	II.8	44	VI.3	53	I.1
9	VI.9	18	V.7	27	IV.3	36	I.5	45	III.7	54	I.7

Synopsis

Ennead **VI.4**

Chapter 1

1–13   What is the relation between soul and extension? In what sense is the soul said to be everywhere in that which it ensouls?

13–29   Comparison of the presence of soul in body and the presence of qualities (forms in matter): the latter are something of the body and divisible along with it whereas the soul is not.

29–34   If the soul can be seen to reach the greatest extension even prior to bodies, it will be easier to see how this can happen also in bodies.

Chapter 2

1–13   The true whole is not *in* anything but the

sensible world is *in* it. The sense of "in" here explained as "resting in" or "depending on."

13–25   The true whole is identical with being which is indivisible.

25–34   What is everywhere in being is also in itself. We, however, (erroneously) placing being in the sensible, come to think of "everywhere" as everywhere in the large bulk.

34–44   The sensible universe "wished to run around" the whole but failed to surround or come inside it. This explains the circular motion of the heavens.

Chapter 3

1–12   Is being present to the sensible by sending powers or by being present itself? If by powers, these powers are not cut off from the source; hence, since being is indivisible, where one power is, all are, but the recipient takes only as much as it is able to.

12–23   The presence of being to sensibles does not mean that being comes to belong to the sensibles and be inseparable from them.

23–35   Being, which is not itself in a place, is present to everything that has a place.

Chapter 4

1–6   How can the previous claims about the unity and indivisibility of being be reconciled with the plurality of beings and souls?

7–18   Response to the objection that the previous claims about indivisibility are paradoxical; we are stuck with the latter view.

18–46 The plurality of beings and of souls is due to otherness which is there prior to any involvement with body.

Chapter 5

1–11   Undiminished giving: the soul constantly gives to extension but is not reduced thereby.

11–22 The terms "large" and "small" do not apply to soul at all in the same quantitative sense as they apply to body.

Chapter 6

1–5   What determines that a given soul does not go to another body? The deeper problem is that the souls are all the same soul.

5–20   Comparison between sense-perception

through different organs within a single ordinary organism and cognitions of different souls.

Chapter 7

1–9   The claim of the previous chapters that each sensible item has a share in one and the same soul is repeated and supported by analogies from the sensible sphere in the remainder of the chapter.

9–22   The power of a hand holding a plank of wood extends to every part of the plank.

22–39   The same light within a transparent, luminous sphere extends to every part of the sphere.

39–47   The same point made with respect to the light of the sun.

Chapter 8

1–22   The conclusions of the previous chapter generalized: that which is not only incorporeal but also immaterial cannot be divided and must be participated in as a whole.

22–45   What has no magnitude cannot be itself present in different magnitudes in such a way as to be divided among them.

Chapter 9

This chapter directly continues the previous discussion but with a change of focus: Plotinus considers several varieties of a hypothesis according to which what comes to be in the many is cut off from its source, and rejects them all.

1–7   The hypothesis that the whole (no doubt soul) is itself parceled into homoeomerous parts, cut off from each other, is refuted.

7–37   Variants of the hypothesis holding that the so-called parts are powers sent off by a transcendent whole are refuted.

37–45   In general, powers or images cannot exist cut off from their sources.

Chapter 10

1–5   Objections to the claim in 9, 37–39: there can be heat in the absence of fire and likenesses such as portraits can exist without their models.

5–17   The case from portraits is refuted.

17–30   The case from fire is refuted.

Chapter 11

1–3   If being (soul) is undivided, why does not everything receive exactly the same, and why is there a difference of rank within the intelligible realm?

3–9   Response to the former question: everything receives according to its capacities, which differ.

9–25   Response to the latter question: the presence of otherness among the intelligibles explains the fact that there may be a difference of rank.

Chapter 12

1–28   Yet another analogy developed to shed light on the mode of presence of soul to body: the way the same word or speech is present to many ears.

28–50   Once again, repetition of the claims that souls do not cease to exist by themselves by ensouling bodies and that whatever participates in the intelligible realm participates in it as a whole.

Chapter 13

1–6   Sense-perception makes us think that the soul is extended.

6–14   Nothing participates in that which it has already got.

14–26   Hence, if the extended participates in anything, it participates in something non-extended.

Chapter 14

1–2   Questions: (1) if soul is the same in every instance, how does each possess his own soul? (2) How is one soul good while another is evil?

2–16   Yet another statement of the unity-in-plurality characteristic of the intelligible realm.

16–31   What are we? We have, even now, our true selves in the intelligible world but in our present state we have become compound.

Chapter 15

1–7   Direct continuation of the end of Chapter 14: a body with a trace of soul approaches the intelligible and receives soul partially even if all is present.

7–40   The degree to which the individual soul succeeds in ruling over the body and its trace of soul varies. This explains how some are good and some are bad.

Chapter 16

1–7   The topic of eschatology and periodic embodiments is introduced.

7–22   The descent of the soul is its coming to be in body without, however, belonging to this body.

22–36   The communion with the body constitutes evil for the soul because it becomes a partial soul and its activity is no longer directed toward the whole.

36–48   The fate of the soul after death. The soul can be freed through philosophy.

Ennead **VI.5**

Chapter 1

1–8   There is a common conception about the god in each of us that holds that numerically one and the same god is present in many.

8–26   This is the firmest principle that our souls proclaim and the same as the universal desire for the good, which is to be found within ourselves.

Chapter 2

1–6   The power of reasoning (*logos*) is twofold, deriving its principles either from the objects of sense or from intelligibles.

6–28   Intelligibles must be studied with the aid of principles that are proper to them. We cannot come to a proper understanding of intelligibles with the kind of reasoning suited to sensible objects.

Chapter 3

1–32   Recapitulation of the main tenets of VI.4 from principles proper to intelligibles: true being is indivisible and unchangeable; it does not leave itself.

Chapter 4

1–13   Given that god is everywhere, god cannot be portioned out like a body with a distinct part of it here, another one there.

13–24   Arguments aiming at establishing that being is present to everything.

Chapter 5

1–23   The center of a circle and radii going from it is introduced as an analogy to the relationship between the One, intelligibles, and sensibles.

Chapter 6

1–6   The intelligibles are "all together," a unity in multiplicity, but in acting on the sensible a partial intelligible becomes active, however containing the whole.

6–15   The intelligible human being makes many sensible human beings but the Idea of a human being is not parceled out on the different human individuals: it is not in the many but the many are in it.

Chapter 7

1–8   We may rise to the level of being. If we do, we are all one and one with the intelligibles and apprehend them directly.

9–17   The reason why we are not aware of our intelligible nature is that we direct our gaze outside and away from them.

Chapter 8

1–22   The participation of Ideas in matter does not involve the multiplication of the Idea.

22–46   The previous point illustrated with thought experiments from the case of the element fire.

Chapter 9

1–13   One and the same agent (soul) produces the whole of the sphere of the sensible cosmos by the whole of itself; one and the same life animates the whole cosmos.

13–23   Previous philosophers' pronouncements about the nature of the soul: quantitative terms do not apply to it.

23–48   The soul is one and many.

Chapter 10

1–11   Eros and lovers of this world are present to beauty itself without receiving it itself.

11–27   Heraclitus' phrase "wise thoughts are common" is expounded.

27–52   The intelligible realm is much more unified than the sensible one in that it is free from the dispersion of spatial extension.

Chapter 11

1–14   The thesis that the soul reaches over a great expanse without being divided is said still to need assurance.

14–38   The intelligible is outside time.

Chapter 12

1–7   The intelligible is inexhaustible.

7–15   We become one with the intelligible whole (being) by being in it without limiting our sight to particulars.

15–29   The intelligible is always present to us but depending on which way we turn our attention we are not always aware of it.

Translation of
Plotinus Ennead *VI.4*

On the Presence of Being, One and the Same, Everywhere as a Whole, Part One

1. Is the reason that soul is everywhere present to the universe that the body of the universe has a certain size, and it is the nature of soul to be "divisible about bodies"? Or is soul everywhere just in virtue of itself, so that it is not just located wherever body may happen to have brought it, but instead body finds | soul to be everywhere 5 prior to it, so that wherever it is put, it finds that soul was already there before it was placed in that part of the universe, and so that the whole body of the universe is placed in an already existing soul? But if the soul extends this far [that is, to the whole space of the universe] even before a body of such a size has come to be there, and if it fills the whole space, how can soul not | have a size? 10 Or how else could anything be in the universe before the

universe has come to be, when there is no universe? And
how could one accept that a thing said to be partless and
unextended is everywhere, if it has no size? But should it
be said to be coextended with body without itself being
15 a body, that too would not let one avoid | the difficulty
by attributing size to the soul accidentally. For in that
case one would still have a good reason to inquire how it
acquires size accidentally. For soul is certainly not present
over the whole of the body in the same way that a quality
such as sweetness or color is. For those are affections of
20 body, so that the whole | of the affected thing has the
affection, and the affection is nothing by itself, since it
is something that belongs to body and it is as such that
it is known. Hence too it necessarily has the particular
extension that it does, and the white of one part of the
body has no community of affection with the white of
another part. And in the case of the white, that belonging
to one part is the same in species as that belonging to
another, but not the same in number, whereas in the case
25 | of soul it is numerically the same thing that is present in
the foot as in the hand, as the phenomena of perception
make clear. And in general in the case of qualities what is
the same is seen to be divided, while in the case of soul
what is the same is not divided, and is only said to be
divided in that it is present everywhere.

     So let us discuss these questions from the beginning,
30 to see whether | we can make it clear and acceptable to us

how the soul, as something incorporeal and unextended, can reach to the greatest possible extension, whether this occurs prior to bodies or only in bodies. Perhaps, if soul can be seen to be capable of such a thing even prior to bodies, it might become easier to accept that this occurs also in connection with bodies.

2. There exists on the one hand the true whole, and on the other the imitation of that whole, the nature of this visible universe. The real whole is in nothing, for there is nothing that is prior to it. But whatever comes after it will of necessity be in the whole, if | it is to exist at all, since it   5
altogether depends on it and without it cannot be either at rest or in motion. And if someone should object that such "being in" is not like being in a place—conceiving of place as either the limit of the surrounding body insofar as it surrounds the thing or as an interval that was previously of the nature of void and still is [when it is filled by body]—but rather | as supported, as it were, by the   10
whole and coming to rest in it, in that the whole exists everywhere and holds it together, let him forget about the application of the term ["being in"] and grasp in thought what is meant.

This has been said for the sake of a further point, namely that that whole, which is also primary and being, has no need of place, nor is it *in* anything at all. Since
| the whole is whole, it cannot fall short of itself but it   15

is filled with itself and equal to itself. And where the
whole is there it is: for it is the whole. Quite generally,
if anything is set into the whole that is different from it,
this participates in the whole and coincides with it and
20 gets its strength from it, not dividing it up, | but finding
it in itself, having come to it, without the whole coming outside itself. For it is not possible for being to be
in non-being, but only, if at all, for non-being to be in
being. Hence it [what is set into the whole] encounters
being as a whole, for, as stated, it is impossible for being
to be drawn apart from itself. And to say that it [being]
25 is everywhere clearly means that | it is in being, so that
it is in itself.

It is nothing remarkable if "everywhere" means
that it is "in being" and "in itself": for to be everywhere
is at this stage to be in a unity. But we place being in the
sensible realm, and so we also place the "everywhere" in
that realm. And since we conceive of the sensible realm
as something large, we are at a loss as to how that nature
30 can extend throughout a thing of so great a | size. But in
fact what we call large is actually small, whereas what we
think of as small is large, if indeed it extends as a whole
to every part of this universe, or rather if this universe
approaches that one from all directions with its parts
and finds it everywhere whole and greater than itself.

Therefore, since it could not grasp anything
35 greater by its | extension—for to do so it would have

had to come to be outside the whole—it wished to run
around it, but since it was unable either to surround it or
to come within it, it was satisfied with having a place and
a status wherein it might be preserved, bordering upon
that whole and present to it, and yet again not present.
For that whole exists by itself, even if something wants to
be present to it. Wherever | the body of the universe may   40
come into contact with it, it finds the whole, so that it no
longer has any need to go further, but instead rotates in
the same place, since what it enjoys as a whole in each of
its parts is indeed everything. For if that other existed in
some place, it would have to approach that place along
a straight line, and would have to make contact with
different parts | of it in different parts of itself, and parts   45
of it would be far from or near to it. But since it is neither
far from nor near to it, that [other] necessarily is present
as a whole, if it is present at all, and it is present to each of
those things that are neither far from nor near to it, those
that are able to receive it.

3. Shall we say then that it [being, the whole] is
itself present, or that it exists in itself and that powers go
forth from it to all things, and that it is in this way that
it is said to be everywhere? For people say that souls go
forth in this way too, like rays, so that it remains fixed | in   5
itself while they are sent out and come to one living thing
and to another. Now, in the case of those things that are

something singular, since the whole of the nature that was there in that thing [being, the whole] is not preserved, a power of it is present to that to which it is present: but even so, this does not mean that the source is not at all present, since even in this case it is not cut off from the

10   po [I] wer which it has bestowed upon the recipient. Yet the recipient was only able to acquire a certain amount of it, even though the whole is present.

But wherever all of its powers are present, it too is clearly present as well; yet even then it is separate. For if it became a form belonging to the recipient, it would then cease to be whole and to be everywhere in itself: it would

15   exist only accidentally and belong to something else. I But as it is, since it belongs to none of the things that wish to belong to it, whereas that which wishes it to be present to it insofar as it is able approaches it, it does not come to belong to the latter—rather the recipient strives after it—nor does it come to belong to anything else either. So there is nothing remarkable in its being in this a way in all things because, again, it is in none of them so as to belong to any of them. Hence there is perhaps nothing absurd

20   either in saying that the soul too runs accidentally I along with the body in this way, if it is said to exist by itself and does not come to belong to matter or to the body, while the whole body is, as it were, illuminated throughout the whole of itself [by the soul].

We should not be surprised if being, which is not

itself in a place, is present to everything that has a place. On the contrary, it would not only be surprising | but 25 impossible to boot if being, while having a place of its own, were present to anything else that had a place, or even were present at all, especially in the way we claim it is. As things in fact are, though, the argument says that it is necessary for being not to have a place and that it is present as a whole to whatever it is present to, and that it is present to the universe in such a way as to be present as a whole to each thing. | Otherwise, part of it will 30 be here and part there, so that it will be divisible, and hence will be a body. For how indeed could you divide it? Will you divide its life? But if the whole of it is life, a part will not be life. Or will you divide Intellect, so that part of it is in one thing and part in another? But then neither part will be intellect. Will you divide its being? | But no part of it will be being, if it was the whole of 35 it that was being. But what if someone says that when a body is divided up, it has parts that are also bodies? But that division was not a division of body, but of a body with a certain size, and each part is said to be a body in virtue of the form according to which it is body, which does not include being of a certain size, nor does it | in 40 any way have a size.

4. How then can there be said to be both being and beings, and many intellects and many souls, if being is

one thing everywhere and not merely the same in species,
and if there is but a single Intellect and a single soul? Yet
the soul of the universe is said to be a different soul from
the others. These considerations seem to count against
5   our thesis, and what | we have said so far, even if it pos-
sesses a certain necessity, still fails to produce conviction,
since the soul finds it incredible that a single thing could
be the same everywhere in this manner. For perhaps it
would be better to divide the whole in such a way as not
to diminish that from which the division has proceeded,
or rather—to use a better expression—to generate from
10   it, and thus to allow the whole to exist by | itself while
those that have come to be, as it were, its parts—that is,
souls—fill out all things. But if that thing, that is, being,
remains by itself—since it seems paradoxical that a whole
could be simultaneously present everywhere—the same
argument will also apply to the case of souls. For they
will not be present as wholes in the whole of the bodies in
15   which they are said to be, but either | they will be divid-
ed, or they will remain as wholes in some particular place
in the body and will bestow from there the power that
they possess. And then the very same difficulty will recur
concerning these powers, about how they can be present
whole everywhere.

     Moreover, one part of the body will possess soul
while another will possess only a power of soul. But how
can there be many souls and many intellects, and how can

there be both being and beings? Indeed, these can be said
to proceed | from their priors as numbers, not as magni-   20
tudes, but they will present a similar difficulty about how
they fill the universe. Thus we have found nothing in this
conception of the proceeding of a multiplicity to help us
resolve the problem. Indeed, we grant that being too is
many in virtue of otherness, not in virtue of place. For
being is "all together," even if in being so it is many as
well, for "being | is next to being," and is "all together,"   25
and intellect too is a multiplicity in virtue of otherness,
not in virtue of place, yet it is all together.

   Then are souls like this too? Yes, they are: indeed,
what is "divisible about bodies" is said to be in its nature
indivisible, but since bodies have size, and since this na-
ture of soul is present to them, or rather since | bodies   30
have come to be located in it, it is, insofar as they are
divisible, and inasmuch as the nature of soul appears to
be present at each part of them, thus conceived as being
divisible about bodies. Yet the fact that it is not parceled
out over the parts of the body, but is whole everywhere,
makes it clear that the nature of soul is really one and in-
divisible. Thus soul's being | one does not do away with   35
the many souls, just as the unity of being does not do
away with the existence of beings, nor does the existence
of multiplicity in the intelligible realm conflict with its
unity. Nor should we say that it is in virtue of multiplicity
that souls fill bodies with life, nor should we think that

the multiplicity of souls comes into being because of the
size of body: rather we ought to conceive soul as being
both one and many prior to bodies. For the many souls
40 are already present | in the whole, not potentially, but
each of them actually. For the unity of the whole soul
does not prevent the many from being in it, nor do the
many prevent the one soul. For they are distinct from one
another without being apart, and they are present to one
another without becoming alien to one another. For they
are not marked off from one another by boundaries, just
as the different sciences that are contained in a single soul
45 are not so distinguished, and | the one soul is such as to
contain all of them within it. For it is in this way that this
sort of nature is unlimited.

5. The greatness of soul should be understood in
this way too, and not like greatness in volume. For that
sort of thing is small, and would be reduced to nothing
if you took away from it, whereas it is impossible to
take away anything in the former case, and even if you
were to do so, it would never be exhausted. But if it can
never be exhausted, why should we fear that it might be
5 absent from anything? | How could it be absent, when
it is never exhausted, but is an "ever-flowing nature,"
which is nevertheless not in flux? For if it is in flux, it
flows forth only as far as it is able, but since it is not in
flux—for it could not be, nor is there anywhere where it

could flow, since it occupies the whole, or rather is itself the whole—and since it is greater than the nature of body, it might reasonably be thought to give only a lit [l] tle to   10 the universe, that is, only as much of it as this universe is able to bear.

We should not say that it [the greatness of soul] is smaller than the universe, nor should we refuse to believe, merely because we conceive of it as being smaller in volume, that in this case the smaller thing is not able to extend over something larger than itself. For we should not even apply the term "smaller" to it, nor should we compare in size a volume with something that is not a volume [l]—for that would be like saying   15 that the art of medicine is smaller than the body of the doctor. Nor, again, should it be conceived as larger in quantitative measure than the universe, nor should the soul be so conceived, for "large" and "larger" in this sense apply [only] to the body. Evidence of the greatness of soul is also the fact that when the volume of a body becomes larger, the very same soul that previously occupied only the smaller volume immediately l extends   20 over the whole. Indeed it would be multiply absurd to add volume to the soul as well!

6. Why then does it [the soul] not also pass to another body? Because that body must, if it is able, approach it, but the body that has already approached it has received

it, and has it. Well then, does the other body have the very same soul in having the soul that it has? In what
5   do they differ? They differ as well | in what is added to them.

Then how is it that the same soul is in the foot as in the hand, while the soul in this part of the universe is not the same as the soul in that part? If the perceptions are different, then we should note that the accompanying affections are different as well. Thus it is the objects being judged that are different, and not the one who judges. The one who judges is the very same judge, who is involved
10   in different | affections. Yet this judge is not the one who undergoes the affections: that is rather the nature of the qualified body. It is as if the same one of us were making judgments concerning a pleasure in our toe and a pain in our head. So why is the one soul not aware of the other soul's judgment? Precisely because it is a judgment, and not
15 | an affection. Nor does the soul making the judgment say "I have judged": it merely judged. Our sense of sight does not say this to our sense of hearing either, even though they were both making judgments, but rather it is our reasoning, which is something different from both, that says this in both cases. And often one's reasoning also sees the judgment made by someone else and has an awareness of the other person's affection. But this has also
20   been discussed | elsewhere.

7. But let us state once more how it is that the same thing extends over everything. This is the same as explaining how each of the many sensible things does not fail to share in the same thing, even though they are dispersed. For it is a consequence of what has been said that it is wrong to divide that one thing into the | many, but instead one must bring the many divided things back to the one. Nor has it gone out to them, but rather, because they are scattered, they have given rise to the opinion in us that it is parceled out with them, as if one were to divide a controlling and containing cause into just as many parts as what it controls.

Yet a hand might control | a whole body, a plank of wood several feet long and something more, and the controlling cause would extend over the whole of it, but it would not be divided into parts equal to what is controlled by the hand: the range of the power, it seems, extends as far as it reaches, while the hand is delimited by its own quantity, not by that of the body that it is wielding | and controlling. And if one were to add an additional length to the body it controlled, and the hand was still able to support it, the power of the hand would control that body too, without being distributed over the various parts of the body. But what if one supposed that the corporeal volume of the hand were removed, leaving behind the | very same power that previously supported the body, the power that before was located in the hand?

Wouldn't the same power still be extended throughout every part of the plank, and yet be undivided?

Indeed, if you were to make a small luminous volume the center of a larger transparent spherical
25 body surrounding it, so that the light | emitted by the inner body shone throughout the surrounding body, and there was no other source of illumination for the outer volume, wouldn't we then say that what is within has spread throughout the outer volume, even though it remains at rest and undergoes no affection, and that the light seen there in the small volume occupies the
30 outer one? Especially since the light is not due to | the small corporeal volume of that body—for it is not *as* body that it came to possess the light, but *as* luminous body, that is, by a different power, and not a corporeal one. Suppose, then, that someone were to take away the volume of the body, but kept the power of the light, would you any longer be able to say that the light had a particular location, or would it not rather be equally
35 present | throughout the whole outer sphere? You would no longer be able to fix your thought on the place where it had formerly been located, and you could no longer say where it came from or where it was going: you would be at a loss about this and would be amazed when you looked and knew the light to be simultaneously present at this and also that point of the spherical body.
40   Moreover, in the case of the sun | you are able to say

where the light originates that illuminates the whole of
the air, in looking toward the body of the sun; nevertheless you see the same light everywhere, without its being
divided. This is made clear by the light being cut off on
the other side of the object than that whence it came: it is
prevented from being there, yet it is not divided. Surely
then if the sun were merely a power | and existed apart   45
from its body and still emitted light, the light would not
come from that place, nor would you be able to say where
it came from, but the light would be one and the same
thing everywhere, and would not begin from or have its
source in any particular place.

8. In the case of light, since it is something that belongs
to body, you are able to say from where it has come, since
you can say where the body it belongs to is located, but if
there is something immaterial which has no need of body,
since it is prior to all body and is established in itself, or
rather | does not even require this sort of establishment,   5
if that thing has that sort of nature and does not possess
any source or place or body from which it began, or body
to which it belongs, how could you then say that one
part of it is here and another there? For then it would
have a place from which it began and it would belong
to something. So we can say only | that if something   10
participates in it, that it participates in it in virtue of the
power of the whole, without it being affected in any way,

and especially not by being divided. For being affected,
even if only accidentally, can happen to something that
has a body, and for that reason such a thing may be said
to be subject to affection and to be divisible, since it is
15   something belonging to body, either as an affection or |
as a form of a body. But a thing that belongs to no body,
but to which body wants to belong, will necessarily be
in no way subject to any of the other affections of body,
and in particular will not be capable of being divided,
since this is a property of body—indeed it is the primary
affection to which it is subject *as* body. But if it is *as* body
that the divisible is divisible, then *as* not being a body, the
20   indivisible will be indivisible. For how | can you divide
it, if it has no magnitude? If then what has magnitude
participates in some way in what does not have magnitude,
it would participate in it without that thing being divided,
or else it will again need to have magnitude.

   Thus whenever you speak of it as being "in many,"
you do not mean that it has itself become many, but you
are attributing to that unity the affection that belongs
to the many, in seeing the same thing as simultaneous-
25   ly present in | many things. The expression "in them"
is to be understood not in the sense that it has come to
belong to each of them nor yet to the totality; rather it
belongs to itself and is itself, and in being itself it does
not depart from itself. Nor is it of the same size as the
sensible universe nor any part of the universe; nor does it

have any sort of | quantity at all. For how could it have   30
a size? Having a size is a property of body: one should
in no way attribute size to anything that does not have
body, but is of a different nature, when one cannot even
attribute quality to it. Hence one must not attribute location to it either, hence no "here and there," for then it
would have location many times over. If, then, | division   35
is something that obtains in virtue of places, that is, when
one part of a thing is in one location and another is in another, how could that to which location does not belong
have the property of being divided? Therefore it must be
indivisible and together with itself, even though the many
may strive to possess it. So if the many strive to possess it,
clearly they are striving to possess the whole of it, so that
if they are indeed able to parti[|]cipate in it, they must   40
insofar as they are able participate in the whole of it. Thus
the things that participate in it must stand in a relation to
it which is such that they do not actually acquire it, since
it is not proper to them. In this way it would be able to
remain whole and by itself, yet also be present whole in
the things in which it is seen. For if it is not whole, it is
not itself, nor again will participation be in the thing that
they are striving for, | but in something else, for which   45
they are not striving.

9. For if the part that came to be in each of them
were a whole and each one itself were like the primary

item, but in each case cut off from it, we would have many
primary items and each of them would be primary. Moreover, what would there be to prevent these many primary
5   things from all together | constituting one thing? For it
is surely not their bodies [that differentiate them], since
it is impossible for them to be forms belonging to bodies,
assuming that they are similar to the primary entity from
which they derive.

But if these so-called parts that are present in the
many are powers of it, in the first place none of them will
any longer be whole. Next, how could they have come
to the many, if in so doing they had been cut off from
10   their source and had left it | behind? For if they have
left it behind, then clearly they have left it at some point
while proceeding. Also, are the powers that have come to
be present here in the sensible realm still present in the
source, or not? For if they are not, we have the absurdity
that the source has been diminished and has lost its
power by being deprived of the powers it previously
15   possessed. And | how could the powers themselves exist
apart from or cut off from their own substances? If they
are both in that [the source] and elsewhere, in this realm
they will be either wholes or parts. But if they are parts,
what remains in the higher realm will be parts, and if they
are wholes, either they will be the same here as there,
without being divided, and we will once more have the
20   same thing everywhere un[|]divided, or else the powers

will have become many, each a whole and similar to one another, so that either the corresponding power will be accompanied by each substance, or else there will be just one power which is present with the substance, while the others are mere powers. However, just as there can be no substance without a power, so there can be no power without a substance, for power | in that realm is an entity   25
and substance, or something even greater than substance. But if the powers that derive from the primary item differ from it in being lesser and dim, like a dimmer light that comes from a brighter light, and there are substances, too, present with these powers, so that there is no power without a corresponding substance, in the case of such powers, | which are the same in kind with one another,   30
it will first of all be necessary to concede that either the same power is everywhere, or if not everywhere, at least that the same power is present whole at every point, without being divided, for instance in one and the same body. But if this is so, why not in the whole universe? But if [divided], then each power will have to be divided to infinity, and | it will no longer form a whole with itself,   35
but it will be on account of this division a lack of power. Secondly, the fact that the power in each location is different will prevent there being consciousness.

Further, just as in the case of a reflection of something, for example the aforementioned weaker light, this cannot exist when cut off from its source—

40   and in general everything that has | its existence from
     something else is a reflection of it and cannot be made to
     exist when cut off from it—nor will these powers which
     have come from it be able to exist when they have been
     cut off from it. If this is so, then wherever the powers are,
     their source will simultaneously be present there also,
     so that once more the same thing will be simultaneously
45   present everywhere as a whole | without being divided.

     10. But if someone should say that it is not necessary
     for the image [*eidōlon*] of something to be dependent on
     its original, since it is possible for a likeness [*eikōn*] to
     exist when the original of which it is a likeness is absent,
     and for heat to remain in a heated thing when the fire
5   is gone, | in the first place, as to the original and its
     likeness, if what is meant is the likeness produced by a
     painter, we will not say in that case that it is the original
     that has produced the likeness, but rather that the painter
     has done so, and we will say that it is not a likeness of
     the painter, not even if he were to paint his own portrait.
     For it is neither the body of the painter nor the form
10   represented that does the painting, | and we ought to
     say that it is not the painter but a particular arrangement
     of colors that produces the likeness. Nor is this the
     production of a likeness or an image in the strict sense,
     as in the case of reflections in water or in mirrors, or of
     shadows—in those cases the image gets its existence in

the full sense from its prior and is generated from it, and   15
it is not | possible for the things it generates to exist when
cut off from it. But they will admit that this is how weaker
powers are generated from their priors.

As for what was said concerning fire: heat should not
be called the likeness of fire, unless one was to say that
fire is present in the heat. But if so, | he will be making   20
the heat not to exist apart from fire.[11] Then too the heat
ceases to exist and the body cools off when the fire has
been removed, even if it does not do so right away. If they
allow the powers too to be extinguished in this way, first
of all they will be saying that there is only one imperishable thing, and they will be making souls and intellect to
be perishable. Moreover, | they will make things that are   25
derived from a substance that is not in flux to be in flux.
However, if the sun were to remain fixed in any given
place, it would provide the same light to the same places,
and if someone were to claim that it was not the same
light, this would imply that the body of the sun was in
flux. That what derives from it [the One] | is imperish-   30
able and that both souls and every intellect are immortal
has been argued extensively elsewhere.

11. But why, if it is whole everywhere, does not everything participate in the intelligible as a whole? And

---

11   The negation (conjectured originally by Ficino) seems required in this sentence: Cf. Tornau *ad loc.*

how is it that in that realm one thing is primary, another
is secondary, and other things follow upon it?

5   We must think that what is present is present according to the capacity of the recipient, I and that being
is present everywhere in being without departing from
itself, and that what is capable of being present is present
to it, and that it is present to it insofar as it is capable of
this, but not locally present—as the transparent is present
to light, while participation in light is different for what
is turbid.

And the primary, secondary, and tertiary items are
10   so in virtue of order, I power and differentiae, not in
virtue of their locations. For nothing prevents different
things from being all together, for example soul and Intellect and the various kinds of knowledge, both greater and lesser. For it is from the same [object] that the
eye sees color, smell [perceives] odor, and another sense
something else, but all of these are together, and not sep-
15   arate from one another. I Is it [being] then something
variegated and manifold? Yes, but what is differentiated
is also simple, and the many are one. For it is a single
yet variegated rational formula [*logos*], and the whole of
being is one thing. For indeed it has in itself the other, and otherness belongs to it—for it certainly does not
belong to non-being. And being is not separated from
20   unity, and wherever being is it has its I unity present with
it, yet the one being also exists by itself. For it is capable

of being present while also existing separately. But sensibles are present to intelligibles in one way—that is, those among them that are present [to intelligibles] and to those intelligibles to which they are present—and intelligibles are present to themselves in another way: indeed body is present to soul in a different way than that in which knowledge is present to soul, and in a different way than that in which one knowledge is present to another knowledge when they are both in the same soul. And body | is   25
present to a body in yet another way than these.

12. Just as when there is a sound of a voice in the air and often also within it an utterance [*logos*] an ear is present and receives and perceives them, if you were to place another ear in the midst of the intervening space, the utterance and the sound of the voice would come to it as well, or rather the ear will come to the | utterance,   5
and many eyes would look at the very same thing and all be filled with the sight of it, even though the thing seen is set apart from them—this happens because the one is an eye and the other an ear; similarly, what is capable of possessing soul will have it, and so too will another, and another, and all of them from the same source. The voice was everywhere in the air not as a single | thing that had   10
been divided, but one and whole everywhere. And in the case of sight, even if the air has the visible form [*morphē*] of the object by being affected, it will have it with-

out its being divided, for wherever the organ of vision is
placed, there it has the form. Not everyone's opinion will
be in agreement with this view, but we have presented it in
order to illustrate the fact that the object of participation
is the same unity for all its participants. It is clearer in
15   the case of voice | that the form [*eidos*] in the air is a
whole, since not everyone would hear the same thing
if the spoken word was not whole in each place and if
each organ of hearing did not similarly receive it whole.
But if even the whole of the voice is not even in this case
extended throughout the whole of the air in such a way
20   that a given part of the voice is joined to a given | part
of the air, so that it is divided into parts accordingly, why
should we think it incredible that the single soul should
not be extended and divided, and that it is everywhere
wherever it is present and that it is everywhere in the
universe without being divided? When soul has come to be
present in bodies, however this may occur, it will be ana-
25   logous to the spoken voice that is already in the | air,
while soul prior to bodies is analogous to the speaker and
him who is going to speak. However, even when it has
come to be in body, not even then has it ceased to exist
in the speaker, since when he is speaking he both has the
voice in him and produces it.

The case of the voice is not the same as that to
which we have compared it, nevertheless there is some
30   similarity. As | for the properties of soul, since it belongs

to the other nature, one must understand that it is not the case that one part of it is in body while another part exists by itself, but rather that it exists whole in itself and only appears to be in many. And when another body comes to receive soul, it obtains from the invisible source the very same thing that was already present in the others. For it is not | as if the soul has been prepared in such a way   35 that a part of soul is located in a certain place and comes forth to this body, but rather what is said to "have come forth" was in everything in itself and is in itself in spite of its seeming to have entered into this realm. For indeed, how could it have come here? So if it has not come here, but is now seen as present, and as present not because it waited for something to participate in it, then clearly | it   40 is present to that thing while also remaining by itself. But if it is present to it while remaining by itself, then that thing has come to it. But if that which lies outside what exists in this manner has come to that sort of being and has entered into the cosmos of life, whereas the cosmos of life exists by itself, then the whole of it [the cosmos of life] exists by itself without being divided up into | its own   45 volume—for there was not any volume—and what has come to it has not come to something that has volume. So that it [bodily nature] does not participate in a part of it [the cosmos of life] but if something else in addition also comes to that sort of cosmos, that too will participate in it as a whole. Similarly, then, if it be said that that cosmos exists as a whole in the things in this realm, it will be in the whole of each of them in the same way. Hence that cosmos will be everywhere, one in | number, not divided, but whole.

13. How then does it extend throughout the heavens and to every living creature? Now, it is not extended: sense-perception, reliance upon which causes us to disbelieve what is said about it, says it exists here and there, but reason says that this "here and there" does not mean that soul has come to be here and | there by being extended, but that the whole of what is extended participates in it, even though it is unextended.

So if something is going to participate in a thing, clearly it will not be participating in itself, else it would not have been participating, but would be that thing. Thus when body participates in something, what it participates in must not be body, for it already possesses that. Hence, body participates in | what is not body. So too size does not participate in size, for it already possesses it. Nor if something should be added to it will the previously existing size participate in size, for a two-cubit length does not become a three-cubit length, but rather a subject which has one size gets another size. Otherwise, the two itself will become three.

Thus | if what is divided and extended to a certain size must participate in something of another kind,

or in general in something different from itself, then that
in which it participates must not be divided or extended
and in general must not be a quantity. Therefore what is
going to be present to it must be present to it everywhere,
without parts, and not without parts merely in the sense
that it is something small: | in that case it will be no less   20
divisible and will not fit the whole of that to which it is
present, nor will the same thing be able to be present to
a thing that is growing. Nor can it be present as a point,
for a volume is not one point, but contains an infinity of
points within it. So it too will have to be present as an
infinity of points, if indeed it is present as a point at all,
and it will not be continuous, so that it will not fit what it
is present to in this way either. So if the whole extended
body is going to possess it as a whole, it will have to pos-
sess it over the whole | of itself.   25

14. But if soul is the same in every instance, how
does each possess his own soul? And how is one soul good
while another is evil?

It suffices also for each, and it contains every soul
and every intellect. For it is infinite as well as one, and all
things are together, and it possesses each as di[|]stinct, yet   5
not as distinguished separately. In what other way could
it be called infinite than this, namely that it possesses all
things together, every life and every soul and every intellect? But none of them are marked off by boundaries, and

for this reason it is also one. For it must not have merely
one life, but an infinity of life, and yet also a single life,
10   and it must have this | one life in such a way that all of
its lives are together, not as aggregated into a unity, but
as having one beginning and remaining as they began. Or
rather they did not begin, but have always existed in this
way, since there is no coming to be in that realm. Nor is
it divided, but merely seems so to whomever so takes it.
15   What is there in that realm is what is ancient and ori[ ]
ginal; what comes to be approaches it, appears to come
into contact with it, and depends upon it.

     But as for us—who are we? Are we the denizens
of that realm, or are we what approaches it and what
comes to be in time? Even before this becoming came
to be, we existed there as different men, and some of us
20   as gods, pure souls and intellect linked | with the whole
of substance, parts of the intelligible realm, not marked
off nor cut off from it, but belonging to the whole.
Nor are we cut off from it even now, but another has
approached that one, another who wants to be another
man. And having found us—for we did not exist outside
25   the whole—he has wrapped himself around us and |
joined himself to the man who each of us then was. It is
as if there was one voice and one utterance, and another
in a different location turned his ear and heard this voice
and received this utterance, and there thus occurred an
actual act of hearing, having what is active present in it.

We have become the compound of the two, not merely
the entity that we were previously, and sometimes we are
the one that we later added to it when the prior entity had
| become inactive and in another way not present.   30

15. But how has what has approached it approached?
Since there is present in it a certain aptitude, it stands
related to that for which it possesses the aptitude. What
has come to be is able to receive soul, but it comes to be
as something not able to receive all soul, even though all
soul is present, though not | to it: just as the other sorts   5
of animals and plants only have as much of soul as they
are able to acquire, as when a sound of the voice signifies
an utterance [*logos*], and some things are able to participate in the utterance along with the sound of the voice,
while others merely receive the voice and its impact.

When the animal has come to be, and has a soul
present to it from being, in virtue | of which it is connected   10
with the whole of being, and there is also present the
body, itself not without a share of soul, a thing that did
not belong even previously to the class of the inanimate,
and that has approached even nearer to soul in virtue of
its aptitude to receive it, and has come to be not merely a
body but a living body, and in virtue of this nearness to it,
as it were, it has acquired | a trace of soul—not a part of   15
soul, but something like a heating or illumination that has
come to it, at this point the generation of appetites and of

pleasures and pains sprung up in it, since the body is not
alien to the animal that has come to be. The soul which
had come from the divine region remained at peace, as it
20   is accustomed to be, and | rested in itself, but the other,
the body, due to its weakness, was disturbed: it was in
flux itself and was struck by blows from things outside it.
It was the body that first cried out to the shared part of
the animal and communicated its own disturbance to the
whole. It is as if a council of elders were sitting in peaceful
25   agreement when an unruly mob arrived, | demanding
food and complaining about the things it had suffered,
so that the whole assembly was thrown into an unseemly
disorder. When such a group is quiet and will listen to the
speech of one who is wise, the multitude becomes peaceful
and orderly, and the worse element does not control it,
30   but if it is not quiet, | the worse element gains control
and the better does nothing, since the noisy multitude
is not able to receive the speech from above. Such is the
vice of a city and an assembly, yet it is also the vice of a
human being, since he has within him a whole populace
of pleasures and appetites and fears which rule over him,
35   that is, when such a man has | bound himself to such a
populace. But whoever enslaves this mob and returns into
himself, that is, into the person he once was, will live the
life of that person and will be that person: he will give
what he gives to the body as to a thing that is distinct
from himself. And someone else will at some times live in

the latter way and at other times in the former, and will thus become a mixture of his good self and | another, evil 40
one.

16. But if that nature [soul] cannot become evil, and if this is the manner in which soul comes into body and is present in it, what about the periodic descent and subsequent ascent of the soul, and the judgments to which it is subject, and its entries into the bodies of other animals? We have taken over these notions from those | thinkers 5
of old who have philosophized best concerning the soul, and it is fitting that we should attempt to show that our present account is consistent or at least not inconsistent with what they say.

Since coming to participate in that nature has turned out to be not for it to approach the things of this realm and to depart from itself, but rather for the nature which exists here | to come to be present in that nature and to 10
participate in it, clearly one must say that what they [the ancients] call its "coming" actually consists in the nature of body entering into that realm and participating in life and soul, and that this sort of "coming" does not involve change of place, but signifies whatever the manner of that communion is. Thus the descent of soul is its coming to be in body—in the way that we claim it | comes to be in 15
body, that is, its giving something from itself to the body, not its coming to belong to the body—and its departure

from body is for the body no longer to have any sort of
communion with soul. And there is a fixed order in which
this sort of communion occurs for the various parts of
this universe, but soul, since it exists, as it were, at the
lower boundary of the intelligible realm, gives of itself
20   to body many times over, since it is near to it in | power
and at a lesser distance from it, in virtue of the law that
governs this sort of nature. But this sort of communion is
an evil for the soul, and its release from it a good.

Why is this? Because, even if it does not belong to
this particular thing, it is still said to be in some way the
soul of it and somehow becomes partial instead of being
the whole. For its activity is no longer directed toward
25   the whole, | even though it still belongs to the whole, just
as when a knower is active with respect to one particular
theorem, even though knowledge is a whole: the good of
the knower does not reside in a part of knowledge, but in
the whole of it that he possesses. So too the soul, though
it belongs to the whole intelligible cosmos and conceals
30   the part in the whole, has as it were leapt forth | from
the whole to the part for that with respect to which it
activates itself is a part—just as if a fire that is able to burn
a whole should be constrained to burn only some part of
it, even though it possesses sufficient power for the whole.
For each particular soul when it exists wholly apart is
not a particular soul, but when it becomes separated off,
though not locally, it becomes the particular in actuality,

and is a portion, not | the whole—though even in this   35
condition it is in another way the whole. When it is not
charged with the care of something, it is altogether whole,
keeping the part, as it were, in potency.

Its coming to be in Hades, if this means existing in
"the unseen," describes its existence apart, but if it means
coming to be in some worse place, what is so surprising
about that? Even as it is now, our soul is said to be wherever
and in whatever place our body happens to be. But what
if | the body no longer exists? If the shade [*eidōlon*] has   40
not been withdrawn from it [the soul], why would it not
be where the shade is? But if philosophy has completely
freed the soul, and the shade has gone by itself to the
worse place, the soul will exist purely in the intelligible
realm, without there being anything dependent on it.
So much for the shade which comes from this sort | 45
of thing; but when the soul, so to speak, is illuminating
itself, it is then concentrated upon the whole in virtue of
its inclination in the other direction, and it is no longer
actual, but nor is it destroyed. So much for these matters;
let us take up again our original discussion.

Translation of
Plotinus Ennead VI.5

On the Presence of Being, One and the Same, Everywhere as a Whole, Part Two

1. A common conception says that there really is such a thing as being one and the same in number simultaneously present as a whole everywhere: everyone is spontaneously moved to say that the god present in each of us is one and the same. And if one did not ask the manner of this, and I bothered to rationally examine 5 their opinion, they would assume that this was so; and in the act of thinking this they would come to rest, fixing themselves somehow upon something one and the same, and they would not want to be cut off from this unity.

Indeed, this is the firmest of all principles, which, as it were, our souls proclaim, I not as a generalization from 10 particulars, but as coming before all particulars, before even the principle that states that all things desire the good. For that principle would be true if it were the case

that all things strove after one thing, and were in fact
one, and their desire was for that unity. For that unity,
15   in proceeding | toward the others insofar as it is able,
would appear to be many, and would even in a way be
many, but the ancient nature and the striving for the
good, that is, for itself, leads it back to a real unity, and
every nature is striving for this unity, that is, for itself.
For this is what the good is for this unitary nature, that
20   is, to belong to itself and to be itself, | and this is for
it to be one. It is in this sense too that it is rightly said
that the good properly belongs to us. Hence there is no
need to seek it outside oneself. For where could it be,
if it fell outside of being? And how could one find it in
non-being? Rather, it is clear that it is in being, since it
is not non-being. But if it is being and is in being, then
25   for each of us | it would be in himself. Therefore we
have not departed from being, but are in it. Nor has it
departed from us. Therefore all things are one.

     2. But reasoning, in attempting to examine that of
which we are speaking, and not being a thing that is one,
but divided, employing for the purposes of inquiry the
nature of bodies and getting its principles from there,
5   has divided substance into parts, | because it considered
it to be like body and was not convinced of its unity,
inasmuch as it did not begin its inquiry from the proper
principles.

But for the inquiry into what is one and fully being we must employ principles that are proper for producing conviction about it, that is, intelligible principles, which apply to intelligible objects and to true substance. For since there is on the one hand | the sort of thing that is 10 in motion and admits all sorts of changes and is always spread out over all places, which would more properly be called becoming than substance, and on the other hand there is being, which is always the same and in the same condition, neither coming to be nor passing away, having no place or location or seat, | neither going forth to any 15 other place nor entering into any other thing whatsoever, but remaining within itself, if one were speaking about the former sort of thing, one might reasonably begin one's reasoning from that nature and what is believed to be true of it, and so through probable reasoning produce probable syllogisms proceeding from probable prem- ises, but when one is giving an account of intelligibles, | the correct procedure would be to employ the nature 20 of the substance with which one is dealing to establish the principles of one's reasoning, without inadvertently passing over to the other nature, and employing that na- ture itself to grasp itself, since in all cases the what-it-is is the starting point of inquiry, and it is said that people who give a good definition of a thing | will also know 25 most of the accidents that hold of it. But in the case where everything is included in the what-it-is, it is all the more necessary to hold fast to this, and to look to it and to refer everything to it.

3. If, then, this is real being, and is "in the same condition" and does not go forth from itself, and it has been said that no coming to be occurs about it and that it has no location, then necessarily, if it is like this, it is always together with itself and does not distance itself 5 from itself, and it is not the case that part of it | is here and part there, nor does anything proceed from it. For if it did, it would be in different places, and more generally would be in something else, and thus it would not exist by itself or be impassible. For if it were in something else, it would be affected, so that if it is in a state of impassibility, it is not in anything else. If, then, it did not become absent 10 from itself or become divided or undergo any sort of | change, yet it was in many things while remaining whole and one with itself, then something that was the same as itself everywhere could be in many things. But this would be for it to exist by itself yet not by itself. The only remaining alternative is to say that it is itself in nothing, but that the others come to participate in it, those that are 15 capable of being present to it, and | insofar as they are able to be present to it.

Accordingly, it is necessary either to do away with these hypotheses and principles by denying that such a nature exists, or, if this is impossible and there necessarily

exists such a nature and substance, one must accept our
original thesis, namely that a thing one and the same in
number, not becoming | divided, but remaining whole, is   20
absent from none of the things that come from it, and has
no need of flowing forth, neither by parts coming forth
from it, nor by itself remaining whole while something
else has left it to come out to the many scattered things.
For in that case it would be in one place, while | what   25
comes from it would be elsewhere, and it would thus have
a place at a distance from those things that derive from it.
And for these too, there is the question of whether each
of them is a whole or a part. If each is a part, it will not
preserve the nature of the whole, as has been said. But
if each is a whole, we will either divide each of them up
into as many parts as there are parts of the original whole,
or else we must concede that the same thing | is able to   30
be whole everywhere. Note that this argument is drawn
from the very nature of the thing itself, without appeal to
anything foreign taken from the other nature.

4. Observe also the following point, if you please.
We do not hold that god is in one place, but absent from
another. For it is believed by all who possess some conception of the gods that one must say, not only concerning god, but also about all the gods, that they are present
everywhere, | and indeed reason requires that we hold   5
this. But if god exists everywhere, then he cannot be

divided, for otherwise he would no longer be everywhere, but each part of him would be located at a different place, and he will no longer be one, as when a magnitude is cut up into many magnitudes: thus god will be destroyed and
10   the collection of his parts will no longer | be the same whole. In addition, god will turn out to be a body. If these consequences are impossible, then what was disbelieved has reappeared: in the entire human nature together with the belief in god comes the belief that the same thing is simultaneously present everywhere as a whole.

Again, if we say that that nature is infinite—for it is
15   certainly not limited—what else could | this mean than that it is never exhausted? But if it will never be exhausted, is that because it is present to each thing? For if it could not be present [to each thing], it will be exhausted, and there would be somewhere where it is not. For indeed, should we say that something else that comes after the One itself is present, this will be together with it, and what comes after it will be around it and directed toward it, and it will be, as it were, an offspring of it and united with it,
20   so that whatever participated | in what comes after it will participate in it as well. For since there are many things in the intelligible realm, things of the first and second and third rank, and it is like a single sphere connected to one point, and these things are not distinguished from one another by intervals, but they are all of them present together to themselves, then wherever the things of the

third rank are present, those of the second and the first rank are present as well.

5. In the interest of clarity, our reasoning has often chosen to employ the example of many lines radiating from a single point to illustrate the notion of the multiplicity that comes to be. But in speaking of the so-called "many" as having come into being, we must be careful to maintain the principle of "all things together," since also | in the example of the center of the circle it is not pos-   5
sible to conceive the lines as distinct from one another, since there is but a single surface.

But where there is not even an interval corresponding to a single surface, but merely unextended powers and substances, it would be reasonable to speak of all things as being at the center, since they are all united together in a single point, as if the end-points of the radii on the | 10
side of the center had let go of their attached lines, so that then all of them would be one. If one were then to once more join the lines to the points, each of the lines would be in contact with the end-points they had left behind, but the end-points would each nevertheless be centers, not cut off from the one original center; each of them will be together with that center, | and there will be as   15
many of them as there are the lines to which they gave themselves as their end-points. Thus, they will appear as just as many as the lines that are in contact with the center,

yet they will all be one. If, then, we liken the many
intelligibles to many points superimposed upon and
unified in a single point, which appear as many because
20 | of the lines, the lines themselves not having generated
them, but merely pointing to them, then let this example
of the lines serve our purposes for the present, as being
analogous to those things which by being in contact with
the intelligible nature, make it to appear as many and as
being in many places.

6. For the intelligibles, though many, are one, and,
though one in virtue of their limitless nature, they are
many, and there are many in one, and one over the many,
and "all are together." And they are active toward the
whole together with the whole, while being active toward
5   the part again together with the whole. The | part
receives into itself the first product of this partial activity,
but the whole accompanies it: it is as if man, in coming to
the particular man, becomes a particular man, while still
remaining man. Thus, from the single man, the Idea, the
10   man that is in matter has made many identical men; | and
the same single thing is in such manner in many, that it is
a single thing as if imprinted the same in many. But man
himself, and each Idea itself, and the whole universe, is
not in many in this way, but the many are in it, or rather
around it. For the way in which white is everywhere is
different from the way in which the soul of each person is
15   the same in every | part of the body, and it is in the latter
way that being is everywhere.

7. Indeed, both we and what belongs to us are referred back to being, and we reach up to that level and the first thing that comes from it, and we think those objects without having images or impressions of them. But if we do not have images or impressions of them, we think them by being them. So if we participate | in   5
true knowledge, we are those objects, not by taking them into ourselves, but rather by ourselves being in them. But since others too, not only we, are those objects, all of us are those objects: and therefore, since we are together, we are those objects with all. Thus we are all one.

Yet since we look outward from the point where we are attached to them, we are unaware that we are one, | like faces that are on the outside many but have but a   10
single head on the inside. But anyone who is able to turn around—either by his own efforts or by the good luck of having Athena pull his hair—will see god and himself, and everything. At first, he will not see himself as all things, but then, since he will not have anywhere to put himself in order to measure | the extent of himself, he will cease   15
marking himself off from the whole of being, and he will come to the whole of everything, without going forth anywhere, but remaining where everything is placed.

8. I think that if one also were to examine the participation of matter in Forms, one might more easily come to accept our thesis and no longer reject it as impossible or raise difficulties about it. For I think it is both reasonable

and necessary, inasmuch as the Forms and Matter are
5   not separate | and apart from one another, that the
illumination of Matter by the Forms does not descend
upon matter from somewhere far above—if indeed this
manner of speaking is not wholly devoid of sense. For what
could "distance" and "separation" amount to in this case?
Furthermore, participation could not be called "difficult
to explain" and "most puzzling," but might very easily be
10   explained | and grasped by means of examples. But even
if we may occasionally use the term "illumination," we do
not mean this in the way we speak of the illumination of a
sensible object by sensible objects; rather, since the things
in matter are images, while the Forms have the status of
archetypes, and the nature of illumination involves the
15   illuminated object being something separate, | it is for
this reason that we speak in this way. But now we must
speak more precisely, and not suggest either that the Form
is separate in location or that the Idea is seen in matter as
if it were a thing reflected in water: instead we must say
that matter, as if it were simultaneously both in contact
and not in contact with the Idea from all directions,
20   acquires throughout itself from the Form in virtue of its |
approach as much as it is able to receive, with nothing in
between them, and without the Idea passing through and
running over the whole of matter, but remaining in itself.

For if the Idea, say, of fire is not in matter—for we
may assume that what we are discussing is the matter that

underlies the elements—then fire itself, without itself
having entered into matter, | will supply the character   25
of fire over the whole of the fiery matter. Let us assume
that the first enmattered fire has become a manifold volume; for the same account will also apply to the other
so-called elements. If, then, that single fire, understood as
the Idea, is seen providing an image of itself in all [fires],
| it will not provide it in the way something separate in   30
place would do so after the manner of a visible illumination. For the whole of this fire would then already be in
the sensible realm, nor could it be many when it itself—
the Idea of it—remained without a place while generat-
ing places from itself, since then the same thing, having
become many, must flee from itself, in order to become
many in this way and to come to participate in the same
thing | many times over. And the Idea gives nothing of it-   35
self to matter, since it cannot be dispersed, nevertheless it
is certainly not unable, given that it is one, to inform what
is not one with its unity, and in this way to be present to
the whole of what is not one, not informing one part with
one part of itself and another with another, but informing each part of it as well as the whole with the whole
of itself. For it is ridiculous | to introduce many Ideas   40
of Fire, so that each fire is informed by a different Idea,
for if so the Ideas will turn out to be infinite in number.
Furthermore, how will you divide up the things that come
to be, if there is but a single continuous fire? And if we

were to add another fire to this portion of matter, so as to
45   make it larger, | we would then be forced to admit that
the same Idea produces the same effects upon this part of
matter as well—for certainly there could not be another
Idea that does so.

9. If continuing with the above account one were
then to say that when all the elements had come into
being they were arranged in the form of a single sphere,
it would be a mistake to claim that a multiplicity of agents
produced the various parts of the sphere, each one of them
marking off a different part for itself to produce: rather
5   one should say that the cause of its | production is one,
and that this cause produces the sphere with the whole
of itself, not that different parts of it produce different
parts. For if that were so, we would once more have many
agents, that is, unless one referred the production to a
single partless cause, or rather, unless what produces the
sphere is a single partless thing that does not allow itself
to flow forth into the sphere, but instead the whole sphere
10   depends | on the thing that produces it. And thus one and
the same life occupies the sphere as well, since the sphere
itself is placed within a single life, and everything that is
contained in the sphere also depends on this single life.
And thus all souls are one, and are one in such a way
that they are also unlimited in number. For this reason
some have declared the soul to be number, others that it

is a ratio that increases its | own nature: they so imagined   15
it perhaps because it cannot in any way be exhausted, but
goes forth over all things while remaining what it is, and
if the cosmos were to extend even further than it does,
the power of the soul would not be exhausted so as not
to be able to reach everything in it—or rather this cosmos would be in the whole of the soul. But we must not
understand the term "increasing" in its literal sense, but
as meaning that | the soul is not exhausted in reaching   20
everywhere while being one.

For its unity is such that it is not susceptible of being
quantitatively measured. For that belongs to a nature that
has a false unity and is imagined to be one only by participation: the unity that attaches to truth is of the sort that
is not composed of many other unities so that when one
of them is removed from | it the unity of the whole is   25
destroyed. Nor is it divided by boundaries, so that if the
others do not fit in it, it is either surpassed by them, if
they are bigger than it, or it is torn asunder in wishing
to extend to all things, and so that it is not present to the
other things as a whole, but only parts of it to the parts of
them, and as the saying goes "it does not know where | 30
on earth it is," since it is scattered from itself and is unable
to unite into some kind of completeness. So if its unity is
a genuine unity, a unity which is capable of having "one"
predicated essentially of it, then it must in a way display
the opposite nature, that of multiplicity, in its potency,

35 in that it does not have this | multiplicity from outside
itself, but has it in itself and from itself. And in virtue
of this fact it is really one and contains both infinity and
multiplicity within its unity.

Since it is like this, it appears everywhere as a whole,
because it is a single rational formula encompassing itself,
and the self-encompassing rational formula is such as to
40 nowhere depart from itself, | but is everywhere in itself.
Since it is so, it certainly is not distinguished from anything by place, for it is prior to everything that is in place
and has no need of those things, but rather they have
need of it in order to have somewhere to be established.
But when they have been established, that thing does not
depart from its own seat within itself, for if it were to
45 move, they would be destroyed, since their foundation |
would be destroyed along with the thing that is responsible for setting them up. Nor is that thing so unintelligent
as to be torn asunder by departing from itself and, when
it is well-preserved within itself, to give itself up to an
uncertain place, a place that itself is in need of it in order
to be preserved.

10. So it chastely remains within itself and could not
come to be in anything else: those other things depend
upon it, as if by their fervent desire for it they have
discovered where it is. And this is the "Eros upon the
doorstep," who is always present on the outside, striving

for the Beautiful and taking joy that | he is able to   5
participate in it in this way. For indeed the lover in this
world too is beautiful not by receiving Beauty but by
staying close to it while the latter remains by itself. And
the many lovers of a single object all desire it as a whole,
and so all possess it as a whole when they possess it, for it
was the whole that they loved. For how could it not suffice
for all of them | since it remains? Indeed it is for this very   10
reason that it does suffice, namely that it remains, and it is
beautiful because it is a whole for each of them.

And indeed wise thought (*to phronein*) is also a whole
for all: whence "wise thought is common," and it is not
the case that some of it is here and some there, for that
would be absurd and would mean that wise thinking
required a place. Nor is wise thought distributed in the
way the color white is, for it is not something that belongs
to | body, but if we can really participate in wise thought,   15
then it must be something that is one and the same and
present as a whole to itself. And we obtain it from that
whole, not by taking away parts of it, nor do I get one
whole and you another, with these two being torn apart
from one another. Senates and councils imitate this,
with their members coming together into one for wise
thought: | each member on his own is feeble in respect   20
of wise thinking, but when they meet together in a unity
in council and in true understanding, they produce and
find wise thought. For what could be able to prevent

the intellect of another from being in the same place?
Rather, we are simultaneously present to one another
even though we do not seem to ourselves to be so. It is
25   as if someone were touching the same thing with many |
fingers and thought that he was touching different things,
or if someone plucked the same string but did not see that
he was doing so.

We should try to conceive how we touch the Good
with our souls, for it is not the case that I touch one Good
30   and you another, with one effluence of it | coming to me
here and another to you there, as if part of the Good was
somewhere up above while another part was down here.
The giver gives to those who receive it not as to alien
recipients, but to those who belong to it, and intellectual
giving is not a matter of sending anything off. Even
35   giving in the realm of bodies that are separated from |
each other in place is also a matter of giving to another
thing belonging to the same kind: giving and producing
occur with respect to the same, and the corporeal part
of the universe acts and is affected within itself: nothing
external to it acts on it. But if in the case of body there
is nothing external to its nature that, as it were, flees
40   from itself, how could there be something external |
in the case of what is unextended? Therefore we are all
present together and we see the Good and touch it being
simultaneously present with our own intelligibles. And
there is much more of a single cosmos in that realm:

otherwise we would have two sensible universes that
are divided into parts, similar to each another, and the
intelligible sphere, if it were one in this way, would
resemble the sensible one, so that it will differ only in
that | it would be more ridiculous, since this sphere   45
reasonably and necessarily has volume, but that one
would extend itself even though it had no need to and
would go beyond itself. And what would prevent them
[the intelligibles] from uniting? For one thing will not
push away another and not yield its place to it, just as
we do not see bits of learning and theorems and more
generally all the branches of knowledge | cramped in the   50
soul. But someone may object that this does not apply in
the case of substances. But it would only fail to be possible
if the real substances were bodily volumes.

11. But how can something unextended reach over
the whole body of such a great magnitude? And how can
it not be torn apart in doing so, even if it remains one and
the same thing? This difficulty has been so often raised
and our reason has been willing to spend excessive effort
to quiet our mind's puzzlement. | Indeed it has already   5
been repeatedly demonstrated that it must be so, but we
still need certain assurances. Not the least but actually
the greatest contribution to confidence is the exposition
of this nature such as it has been expounded, namely, that
it is not like a stone—like some great block of stone, lying

where it is and occupying a certain amount of space, not
10 being able to exceed | its own boundaries, measured as
being just the quantity that it is both by its volume and
by the power of the stone that is contained within this
volume. Rather, since it is the primary nature and is not
measured in respect of the quantity it must be—for if it
were, it would have to be measured by another nature—
it is all the power there is, and is in no way limited in
quantity.

15   For this reason, it is not in time, but lies | wholly
outside time, since time is always being dispersed into extension, but eternity remains within itself and governs itself and in virtue of its eternal power is greater than time
which seems to go on so far: it is as if a line that seems to
go on to infinity is attached to a point and rotates around
20 that point, | so that everywhere the line goes, the point
is seen to be present upon it, though the point itself does
not move, but instead the line rotates about the point. If,
then, time stands in an analogous relation to that which
remains fixed in its substance, and that nature is unlimited not only in that it is everlasting but also in respect
25 of its power, we must then declare that related to this |
infinity of power there is another nature that runs along-
side it, hanging from and depending upon it, and that
this nature goes on just as far as time does, compared
to the nature that is fixed and remains, which is greater
than it in virtue of producing it, and whatever it is, it is

as it were stretched out against that nature, being what participates in it insofar as | it is able to do so, with the   30 whole of that nature being present, but not being seen as a whole at every point of it in virtue of the weakness of the substrate. It is present numerically the same at each point, not in the way that the enmattered triangle is many in many subjects, but in the way that the immaterial triangle, from which the triangles in matter are derived, is the same thing. But why is the material triangle not | 35 everywhere, if the immaterial triangle is everywhere? Because not every matter participates in it, but each portion of matter possesses something different, and every matter is not related to everything [every Idea]. Not even the whole of prime matter is related to every Idea, but only to the primary kinds, while others are related to these. But there is something [of the whole] present to every matter.

12. How, then, is it present? As a single life. For the life in an animal is not just present up to a certain point and from there on unable to reach to the whole of it, but it is present everywhere. If someone again asks how this is possible, let him recall what was said above concerning its power, that it is not a definite quantity, but that even if he divides it to infinity in | thought it will always possess   5 the same power, infinite all the way down. For there is no matter in that realm which would cause its magnitude to be exhausted along with its volume as it gets smaller.

So if you now should take hold of an ever-flowing
infinity that is contained within it [the life], a nature in
itself tireless and indefatigable, in no way falling short of
itself, like a life boiling over, you will not find it there by
10   gazing somewhere | or staring at something particular.
Quite the opposite will happen to you: for neither will
you miss it in passing nor, again, end up experiencing it
as small as though it could no longer give by falling short
in terms of smallness: either you are able to run along
with it, or better: you will come to be in the whole, and
no longer seek anything, or else you will give up and will
15   pass from it to something else and you will falter, | failing
to see what is present because you are looking at something else.

But if you no longer seek anything, how does this
happen to you? It is because you have come to the whole
and did not merely remain in a part of it; you did not say
"I am this much," but you abandoned the "this much"
and in so doing you became the whole. Yet, even before
20   this you were the whole, but because there was also |
something else present in you besides the whole, you
were diminished by the addition, since the addition did
not come from being, for you can add nothing to that,
but from non-being. Anyone who is constituted from
non-being as well [as being] is not the whole, but is so
only when he abandons non-being. So you will increase
yourself by abandoning other things, and if you abandon

them, the whole will be present to you. | But if it is present 25
when you abandon them but does not appear together
with them, it follows that it did not come to you in order
to be present, but you departed at the moment when it
was not present. But if you departed, it was not from it
that you departed—for it is still present—nor did you
even depart then, but rather though present you turned
away from it to what is its opposite. For similarly other
gods too often appear only to one person | though there 30
are many people present, because only that one person
is able to see them. But these are the gods who "in many
forms travel around the cities," while cities themselves
turn toward that god, as does the whole earth and the
whole of the heaven, that god who everywhere remains
by himself and in himself and possesses from | himself 35
being and the things that truly exist, down through soul
and life: these things depend on him and proceed by
virtue of his sizeless infinity toward his infinite unity.

Commentary on
Ennead *VI.4*

Title

On the Presence of Being, One and the Same, Everywhere as a Whole

Porphyry, Plotinus' ancient editor, provided the titles of his treatises that they still bear. In this case the title is inspired by Plato's *Parmenides* 131b1–2 and 144c8–d1. In some respects the title can be said to indicate the content of the treatise accurately but it may mislead in that it does not mention soul, which is the main topic of the treatise.

Chapter 1

This chapter introduces the main question of VI.4–5: How is soul related to extension?

1, 1–13 *Is the reason . . . has no size*: Plotinus begins this first chapter by raising questions concerning the relation between soul and extension that are going to occupy him for much of the remainder of the treatise. He takes it as given that the soul as such is incorporeal and unextended. It is equally given that the soul is everywhere in the body it ensouls. This constitutes a problem: how can something in itself unextended reach over a body, even the enormous body of the universe, as the World-Soul does? He has briefly discussed such issues in earlier treatises, IV.2 [4] 1 and IV.1 [21][12] but apparently felt that a more thorough treatment was needed. In 1–8 he presents two alternatives for how the soul can be said to be everywhere: (1) it is because body is of such and such size and it is the nature

---

12   The relative dating of IV.1 is uncertain (cf. Strange [1992, 482 note 10]). It can be presumed to predate our treatise, however.

of the soul to be divided along with the body; (2) it is because the soul is everywhere prior to the body.

In the background of the question is the statement in *Timaeus* 36d2 that the World-Soul extends throughout the sensible universe and the statement in the account of the genesis of the World-Soul in *Timaeus* 35a2–3 that the soul is "divisible about bodies." This is a passage Plotinus very frequently refers to and seeks to interpret in such a way that it doesn't claim the soul to be essentially divisible into spatially distinct parts. On Plotinus' reading of *Timaeus* 35a see Schwyzer (1935) and Morelli (2011).

Plotinus may intend "coextended" in 14 to be equivalent to "divisible about bodies" in 2–3, in which case we would see the first question addressed in 13–17. The second question gives rise to further questions. To say that the soul is everywhere prior to the body of the universe seems to attribute size to it: it must be at least as extended as the universe if it is there prior to the universe (8–10). Furthermore, how could anything be present in the space of the universe prior to the universe (10–11)? These questions seem to presuppose that extension came to be at some point in time, a view Plotinus does not endorse (cf. II.1.1; Wilberding [2006, 41ff.]). As will become clear in the next chapter, Plotinus does not accept the presuppositions of these questions. It is, however, not the presumed temporal beginning that he will question but rather the meaningfulness of ascribing to anything intelligible terms such as "everywhere" and "in" in the sense in which such terms apply to bodies. Finally, he asks how something said to be partless and unextended can be everywhere (11–13). That the soul is indivisible and unextended is, with certain qualifications, something Plotinus consistently holds. As Tornau (*ad loc.*) suggests, "said to be" indicates that Plotinus has a Platonic passage in mind, presumably here *Timaeus* 35a.

1, 13–17 *But should it . . . acquires size accidentally*: Here Plotinus considers as a possible solution that the soul, though not a body itself, nevertheless is extended along with the body and thus has size accidentally. That the soul is accidentally extended is a view Nemesius attributes to Numenius and to Plotinus' teacher Ammonius Saccas (*On the Nature of Man* 18.15–22 = Numenius, fr. 4b). Plotinus claims that this does not dispel the problem, we need to know how the soul is accidentally extended. This leads him to the comparison that follows in 17–29 between soul and forms (*eidē*) in matter or qualities such as colors and sweetness, which is supposed to show that the qualities are coextensive with the body they qualify and may be said to have size accidentally. He concludes that the case of the soul is quite different from that of the qualities. He does admit later (4.3, 19–20) that in a

sense the soul can be said to be accidentally extended
("runs accidentally along with the body" is the expression
there) but that sense is different from the sense in which
qualities are accidentally extended.

1, 17–24 *For soul is . . . same in number*: Here Plotinus
develops the distinction between the way qualities (forms
in matter), on the one hand, and soul, on the other, are
related to bodies. In the case of the white, for example,
the same form is clearly present in many bodily parts: this
part is white, so is that other one. However, the white in a
body has no independent existence and is just something
of the body (20–21); hence, it partakes in its extension
and, for instance, the white in one part of the body is
a numerically different item from the white in another
part (21–23; cf. IV.2.1, 33–40). The soul, by contrast,
is numerically the same in the different parts. This
distinction is of great importance in the treatise. Plotinus
will repeat, almost *ad nauseam*, that the soul, despite its
embodiment, does not come to belong to the body or
share in its dispersion into different parts.

It emerges from the account here that there is a certain
order of ontological levels: souls, forms in matter
(qualities of bodies), mere bodies. This is an order from
greater to less unity. We see this same hierarchy more
systematically and explicitly laid out in IV.2.1. There

Plotinus defines mere bodies as ". . . things which are primarily divisible and by their very nature liable to dispersion: these are the things no part of which is the same as either another part or the whole, and the part of which must necessarily be less than the whole. These are the perceptible sizes and masses, which each have their own place, and it is not possible for the same one to be in several places at once" (IV.2.1, 11–17). These "primarily divisible things" are shortly afterward in the same chapter identified with bodies (IV.2.1, 33). This understanding of the nature of bodies underlies these lines in 4.1 and in fact our treatise as a whole. In addition, we have in our treatise the notion of pure matter, which is even more "many" than the bodies (see 5.8 and Introduction).

1, 24–29 *Whereas in the . . . is present everywhere*: That the very same soul is present in different parts of the body it animates is evident from facts about sense perception. In the earlier treatises IV.2 [4] 2 and IV.7 [2] 6–7 he argues for this in quite some detail both with respect to the external senses and the internal sense of pain. He clearly believes that the evident fact that one and the same subject can simultaneously be aware of, e.g., a pain in the finger and a pain in the toe shows the undivided presence of the same entity at different locations. In contemporary parlance this can be described as a view holding that the unity of consciousness is incompatible with materialism (the view that everything is a body or bodily qualities). For discussions of these passages, see Emilsson (1988) and (1991).

1, 29–34 Plotinus announces a fresh start: if it can be seen that even prior to bodies the soul can reach the greatest possible extension, it will be easier to grasp how this happens also in bodies.

Chapter 2

The true whole, which is the same, has being, is in nothing, is undivided, and everything that participates in it participates in it as a whole.

Despite the announcement of a fresh start on the same problems at the end of the previous chapter, in this chapter Plotinus seemingly turns to something entirely different: at least it is not obvious how what he does here is a new take on the previous problems. He asserts the existence of the real whole and its imitation, the sensible universe: since there is nothing prior to the real whole, the real whole is *in* nothing, whereas whatever is posterior to it, is *in* it. That Plotinus should change the topic abruptly and radically right after announcing a continuation at the end of Chapter 1 seems even less likely when we consider the fact that the division into chapters is Ficino's from the 15th century and has no ancient authority. As is argued in the Introduction, the radical shift is only apparent: the true whole that Plotinus here introduces comprises soul, which is a true member of the intelligible realm.

His strategy is to consider and establish the nature of the realm to which the soul belongs in order to infer from this what must hold for any soul: even if he has a number of things to say about this whole and the other members of it, it is soul that is his primary concern in this treatise. Thus, he is not radically changing the topic but rather discussing the soul obliquely as a member of the intelligible realm and together with other members of it.

The term "the true whole" here certainly refers to what Plotinus often calls "the intelligible" or "(real) being." It refers to that whole intelligible realm of which souls are also genuine members (see Introduction). That he so regards souls is evident throughout our treatise. One may wonder whether "the whole" even comprises the first principle, the One. Presumably it does not, because in the following discussion it is clear that the sphere Plotinus is talking about is somehow multiple and he also identifies it with being, which we know from elsewhere to be below the first principle. He does say, however, that this true whole is in nothing in the sense of depending on nothing. But if it does not comprise the One, one should think that it must depend on the One. If it does, how can it depend on nothing? We leave this question unanswered.

Plotinus' choice of the word "whole" for the intelligible realm here may reflect the emphasis he puts in our treatise on the unity of this realm. It is a tightly knit web in which each item somehow presupposes or implies every other. This is why he finds an analogy with the sciences, their branches and theorems, so apt to describe the closely knit web of the intelligible: it is a system like that of an overarching science, containing branches and particular theorems, and constituting a system in which the very content of each "part" is determined by its place and relation to the others. A clear expression of this holistic view is to be found in Chapters 4, 6 and 7 of V.8, "On the intelligible beauty." As to the science analogy see especially VI.2.20 and IV.9.5, 12ff., and also in this treatise 4.4, 44–45; 4.16, 32–36, as well as Tornau (1998), and Emilsson (2007, ch. IV, sec. 4).

2, 1–6 *There exists on . . . or in motion*: Plotinus first asserts that the true whole is in nothing, whereas whatever is posterior to it is in it. The sense of "posterior" here is certainly not temporal but logical or ontological. To say that B is posterior to A normally indicates in Plotinus that B is derived from or depends on A. Thus, given the sense of "being in" as "depending on," "resting in," it is a mere truism to say that what is posterior to the true whole is in it.

2, 6–13 *And if someone . . . what is meant*: The views of place referred to in 7–9 are the Aristotelian and the Stoic

views, respectively: Cf. Aristotle, *Physics* 4.2.209b1–2 and
4.212a5–6; Simplicius, *In Aristotelis Physicorum libros
commentaria*, 571, 27–31 = SVF 2, 508. Plotinus explains
that the way he uses the expression "being in" deviates
from the (standard) sense of "being in a place": "being
in" is here used in the sense of "resting in" or "depending
on." For more on this understanding of "being in" and
other points made in the present chapter, see O'Meara
(1980).

2, 13–22 *This has been . . . be in being*: The true whole
is identical with being (*to on*). We see here the first
occurrence in the treatise of the word "being" used to
refer to an aspect of the intelligible realm. In this treatise
"being" is usually used coextensively with the intelligible
realm: all of it is being, which then has becoming, image,
or non-being as contrast terms. The true whole is *in*
nothing in the previously established sense of depending
on nothing. Furthermore, the whole, being whole, in no
way falls short of itself, i.e., it is in no way not whole,
i.e., wherever it is, it is undivided as a whole (13–17).
Whatever is in the whole, i.e., depends on the whole,
participates in the whole, and, which is the same, in
being. Hence, whatever participates in being, participates
in it as a whole (17–25). On the notion of participation
in our treatise see Strange (1992). "Non-being" in 21–22
does of course not refer to absolute non-existence but to

something that is not being in the full unqualified sense in which the intelligible whole is being. So bodies and the sensible realm generally would count as non-being in this sense.

2, 22–27 *Hence it encounters . . . means in a unity*: If the true whole is the same as being and if being "is not drawn apart from itself" (23–24), i.e., is an indivisible unity, clearly what is set into the whole is set into being as a whole. The following lines are difficult, especially 26–27, "for to be 'everywhere' is at this stage to be in a unity." Plotinus has said (25–26) that there is nothing surprising about being being everywhere meaning that being is in being (and hence in itself). The difficult sentence that follows is supposed to explain this. The thought behind the translation here is that at this stage, i.e., the sphere of being, to be everywhere must mean to be in a single unitary thing, i.e., being.

2, 27–34 *But we place . . . greater than itself*: We ordinary humans, however, (erroneously) placing being in the sensible, come to think of "everywhere" as everywhere in the large bulk of the sensible realm. Hence, we are puzzled about what we conceive as "small" (i.e., the whole/being, which is without size) as being everywhere in this large bulk; however, as a matter of fact it is this "small" thing which is truly "large" because when the sensible universe approaches it with any of its parts, it finds it everywhere as a whole. That the intelligible is in an important sense "larger" than the sensible is well known from the previous Platonic tradition (cf. Plutarch, *Platonicae quaestiones* 3.2.1002 B–E).

2, 34–49 *Therefore, since it . . . to receive it*: These lines give Plotinus' explanation of the circular motion of the sensible universe. It "wished to run around" the whole but failed to surround it or come inside it. It therefore had to be content with an eternal circular motion, a kind of compromise between its desire for unity and its own nature. The general idea is the Platonic-Aristotelian one that circular motion is the best thing matter can do to imitate the unchanging intelligible realm. (Cf. Plato, *Timaeus* 33d3–34a7; Aristotle, *Metaphysics* 12.8.1073a26ff.; *On the Heavens* [*De Caelo*] 1.2; 2.3–6; *Physics* 8.8–9). On desire and circular motion in Plotinus see further Wilberding [2006, 66–67].)

Plotinus here attributes a psychological act of wishing to the sensible realm as such. Such ascriptions are in fact very common at all levels of the Plotinian ontological hierarchy except of course the highest, the One: every subordinate level, lacking self-sufficiency, desires the level above. Even matter does this in some sense (cf. 5.8.18–20 and Commentary). Usually the result is similar to what we see here: there is partial success. The lower indeed receives something from the higher which quenches its desire but it fails to become one with its source. Are we to understand talk about "wishing" or "desiring" in contexts like this one literally or purely metaphorically? Surely, it cannot be a question of wishes or desires quite in the way human beings wish and desire. Presumably, what Plotinus has in mind is so far removed from human desires and wishes that his words must be given a metaphorical sense.

The phrase, "those that are able to receive it" is the first reference to the doctrine of reception according to the capacity or the suitability of the recipient (for which see Commentary 4.3, 6–12 and Introduction, Section 3).

Chapter 3

The nature of the presence of being to the sensible.

3, 1–6 *Shall we say . . . and to another*: Is it the case that being remains by itself but sends the souls off as powers, like rays, that come to be present in living beings, as some say? The expression "by itself" (*eph' heautou*) here suggests the image of spatial isolation: the contrasting term is "belonging to body" in 1, 21 (cf. Tornau *ad loc.*). There is no denial of a presence of being to the sensible realm implied, just that being does not cease to exist in its own right by being so present.

Who are the people who compare the souls with rays? As Tornau notes *ad loc.* some Gnostics held views of this sort and it may well be them he primarily has in mind. He may, however, also have in mind Numenius, a 2nd century Platonic-Pythagorean thinker Plotinus was accused of plagiarizing (cf. Porphyry, *Life of Plotinus* [*Vita Plotini*] 17.1ff.). According to Numenius, human beings exist by participation in a divine intellect that descends from heaven, and our bodies are ensouled by the "rays" (*akrobolismos*) that issue from the second or demiurgic god when he is "turned toward" or "looks" at us (cf. Numenius, fr. 12, 17–19).

3, 6–12 *Now, in the . . . it is separate*: In these lines Plotinus connects four central tenets: (1) the view that powers are not cut off from their sources (9–10); (2) the indivisibility of being (8–9); (3) the doctrine of reception according to the capacity of the recipient (10–11) and, finally, (4) the separation (independence, transcendence) of the intelligible source (12). He rejects any view of powers entailing a severance between the power and its source: if powers from being are present to the recipient, these powers are not cut off from being. And if they are not cut off, each power contains the whole. This expression, "not cut off from," occurs several times in the *Enneads*. It is Aristotelian in origin: Aristotle uses it to express the view that the activity of an agent is realized in the patient, e.g., the activity of the teacher is in the pupil who learns (cf. *Physics* 3.3.202b8). Furthermore, it follows from (1) and (2) that even if certain powers may be present to a recipient, where one power is, all are, and where all its powers are, being is present as a whole (11–12). It goes together with such a view that the differences in the outcome must be explained by an appeal to differences in the recipients insofar as they receive each according to their own nature and capacity (3), even if everything is present (10–11). This last qualification is important because it shows that "presence" and "reception" are not exactly correlative: some aspect of being may be present to a recipient even when the latter is unable to receive it in the sense of being somehow altered by this presence. Plotinus does, however, not stick rigidly to this distinction between presence and reception in our treatise: sometimes he talks as if a body's presence to the intelligible is the same as the body's reception (see, e.g., 4.11, 6–7). For this doctrine about reception according to the capacity of the recipient, see Introduction, Section 3.

3, 12–23 *For if it . . . by the soul*: Plotinus proceeds to emphasize that the presence of being to sensibles does not mean that the being comes to belong to the sensibles and be inseparable from them. If it did, it would become like a bodily form and become divisible along with the parts of the body (cf. Commentary 4.1, 25–29). Since it belongs to none of the things that receive it, there is nothing remarkable about its being everywhere present as a whole to all of them. Given this we can see in what way the soul may be said to be accidentally extended through the body it ensouls (19–22): it does not belong to the body but the whole body is illuminated by one and the same undivided soul. Thus it may be said to be accidentally extended in the sense that every part of the body is present to the same undivided soul. On "accidentally extended" see above Commentary 1, 13–29. Clearly, the way in which Plotinus thinks soul can be said to be accidentally extended along with the body in 19–22 is different from the way in which corporeal forms are: the latter belong to the body, the soul does not.

There is a textual problem in 15–16, where HS$_2$ mark a few phrases as unclarified. The translation here follows Tornau's suggestion *ad loc.* to supply the words, *pareinai, ekeinō*, "present to . . . it."

The mention of soul in 20 is one of many instances in the treatise of Plotinus where he moves without warning from talking about being to talking about soul. These cases show first of all that he considers souls as included among beings and further that the soul is the kind of being he is primarily concerned with here. Soul is the only kind of being about which the question of its relation to spatial extension arises (see further Introduction, Section 6).

3, 23–35 *We should not . . . that was being*: Plotinus argues that "being, which is not itself in a place, is present to everything that has a place." The argument seems to be that if being were in a place, it would have one part here, another part there; hence, it would be divisible; hence, it would be body. But it is not body and is indivisible;

hence it is not in a place. Nevertheless, being is present to the sensible, but given its non-spatial nature it must be present as a whole to whatever it is present to. Spatial divisibility is a hallmark of bodies, as is evident from 30–31.

3, 35–40 *But what if . . . have a size*: In these final lines of the chapter, Plotinus raises and rejects an objection to what he has just maintained. Fully spelled out the objection seems to be: "You have just said that no matter how you divide body, you will find the whole soul in every part; but one could say the same about body: a part of a body is also just as much a body as the whole body is." Plotinus' answer (with additions not explicit in the text) is: "True, but that is because the whole and each part have the form of body; corporeal forms can surely be instantiated in many things, even if each of the many is a numerically different item from any other (cf. 4.1, 24); strictly speaking, however, it is only a certain quantity, a body of a certain size, that is divided; division of quantities does not yield parts equal to the divided whole."

Chapter 4

The compatibility of the previous claims about the indivisibility of being with a plurality of beings. Refutation of a view claiming that souls are separated from being. Unity and plurality in the intelligible realm.

4, 1–6 *How then can . . . in this manner*: In the previous chapters the thrust of Plotinus' arguments has been towards the unity and indivisibility of the intelligible realm, including soul. In the present chapter he asks if he may have gone too far: if the intelligible realm, including soul, is so unified and indivisible, how can we accommodate this with common-sense opinions and Platonically sanctioned views about the multiplicity of the intelligible, including soul? Thus, Plotinus points out (3–4) that there are (according to Plato) both the soul of the universe and individual souls (cf. *Timaeus* 41d4–e1). And Plato speaks of being and also of beings (cf. *Parmenides* 144bff.). This is part of the second hypothesis of the *Parmenides*, which for Plotinus describes the sphere of being or Intellect. Indeed, Plotinus himself fully endorses the plurality of both souls and beings, the problem is how to reconcile this with their unity which he also believes in.

In 4–6 he notes that even if his previous arguments yield necessary conclusions, they may fail to carry conviction. Much of what follows, not just in this chapter, but in the rest of the treatise too, is clearly intended to bring about the needed conviction. Similar concerns about persuasion that may be lacking despite conclusive arguments are to be seen later in the treatise (see 4.7; 5.2; 5.11, 6–7).

4, 7–18 *For perhaps it . . . power of soul*: These lines mostly respond to the claim that the undivided presence of soul to the body is paradoxical. Plotinus here considers a revision of his previous claim about such undivided presence and seeks to show that undivided presence is unavoidable, also on the revised account. The argument that follows is somewhat unclear and elliptical. Clearly, though, the idea is to show that this suggestion does not solve any problem, we are left with the paradoxical notion in any case. Here is how we propose to reconstruct the argument, much aided by Tornau's commentary:

Let being remain "by itself," and let the souls be generated from it as its parts though without diminishing it (7–11). This is the revised alternative. The phrase "by itself" is here to be taken in the sense of not entering into any relation with the sensible so as to belong to it (cf. 3, 1–2 and Commentary). Then the same problem recurs with respect to the souls that have entered the body: Either these souls will be divided into numerically different soul parts, which is contrary to the facts (cf. 1, 24ff. and Commentary) or they remain undivided at some point of the body and send forth powers to the rest. In the latter case, the same problem will recur with respect to the powers: They are either undividedly present, the view we must accept, or divided along with the body, which Plotinus again takes to be incompatible with obvious facts. So, the same problem will arise with respect to the individual soul and its relation to its body. Undivided presence will again turn out to be unavoidable. And if it is unavoidable in the case of singular organisms, there is surely no reason for rejecting it for the universe at large.

4, 18–23 *But how can . . . resolve the problem*: Here Plotinus returns to the issue raised at the beginning of the chapter, namely, given what has been asserted in Chapters 2 and 3, how can there be many souls and many intellects? As a possible solution Plotinus mentions the generation of beings and souls from "their priors as numbers, not magnitudes" (19–20). This theory may indeed explain how there can be intelligible plurality without partition of a spatial magnitude (cf. Aristotle's criticism of Plato's account in the *Timaeus* in *On the Soul* [*De Anima*] 1.3.407a8ff.). Plotinus expresses this view also at V.1.4, 6ff., stating that the Ideas and souls are numbers, deriving from the One and the indefinite dyad (cf. also 5.9, 13–14). In the background of Plotinus' thought here is presumably Xenocrates, who defined soul as "a self-moving number" (fr. 60), and Aristotle's account of Ideas as numbers in *Metaphysics* 1.13 and 9. It should be noted that Plotinus distinguishes between ordinary "quantitative" numbers and ideal numbers. It is the latter that are at stake here (cf. the treatise "On Numbers," VI.6.9, 34–37). Plotinus is here following a venerable old tradition. It cannot be said, however, that the identification of Ideas or souls with numbers plays a very prominent part in the *Enneads*: except for the treatise on numbers, which in some respects is unrepresentative, and a few other passages, there are no traces of it. His attitude to this number theory falls short of a full committal and he notes that it does nothing to explain how the souls fill the universe (20–21). Souls as numbers are also mentioned in 5.9, 13ff.

4, 23–26 *Indeed, we grant . . . is all together*: Plotinus first considers the case of intelligible being and beings, then that of souls, but his answer is essentially the same in both cases: the difference between beings and between souls is not a quantitative difference. They differ by otherness, not by spatial location. The notion of otherness here comes from Plato's *Sophist* 254cff. Plotinus considers the five highest genera that Plato invokes in the *Sophist* to be the highest Forms of the intelligible world. The fullest account of this view is to be found in VI.2.1–8. Plotinus does not explain here the exact role otherness plays in constituting plurality in the intelligible realm. The important point remains, however, that there can be truly different things that do not differ by virtue of location, but their own intelligible content as, e.g., the numbers do. On Plotinus' use of the five genera see Brisson (1991) and Santa Cruz (1997).

The beings are "all together" (*homou pan* or *pan homou*) (24; 25). Plotinus uses this or similar phrases very frequently to describe the intelligible realm. In this treatise see 4.14, 4 and 6; 5.5, 3–4; 5.6, 3. What Plotinus has in mind is first of all that the intelligibles are not spatially dispersed. Secondly, Plotinus' holism about the intelligible realm is also implied (see Commentary 4.4.2). This phrase in Plotinus is commonly referred to Anaxagoras B1 but "all together" also occurs relevantly in *Parmenides* B8, 5 which is the likelier source for Plotinus, although he may be alluding to both. The phrase in 24–25, "being is next to being," comes from Parmenides B8, 25. Not infrequently Plotinus approvingly cites Parmenides the philosopher, especially these words and B3. In V.1.5 he praises Parmenides' views on the One but notes that he did not have the full account of the three hypostases. In these lines the unity-in-multiplicity Plotinus wishes to maintain about the intelligible realm is more asserted than argued for or explained.

4, 26–46 *Then are souls . . . nature is unlimited*: Here Plotinus turns to souls. Their unity presents a more difficult case than that of transcendent beings because souls are more separated from one another than the pure intelligibles that have no direct relation to the sensible realm. Moreover, Plato says in the celebrated passage about the generation of the soul in *Timaeus* 35a2–3 that it is "divisible about bodies," cited in 27 (cf. 4.1, 2). Yet, Plotinus insists that this Platonic passage means that the soul, by nature indivisible, is said to be divisible only in the sense that the body, which is divisible, is in the soul in all its parts and hence the soul is present at every part of its extension (28–32). This does not imply that the soul is "parceled out" (32–33). It *appears* to be divided, i.e., to be located at different places in the body, but is actually indivisible. Plotinus then goes on to give essentially the same account of souls as of beings. They too are many prior to body just like beings (39). Thus, the plurality of souls is not due to the souls' presence to extension: the souls are different prior to entering into a relation to bodies (37–39).

In 3 he asks how there is "a single Intellect and a single Soul" and later in the chapter, 34–36 and 41–46, he brings up his view that despite the plurality of souls, beings and intellects, there is one Soul that all the souls are, one Intellect that all the intellects are. He doesn't, however, seriously enter into an argument for this apparently strange view here. There is an early treatise devoted to the question of the unity of all souls, IV.9 [8] "Whether all souls are one," and the idea that, even if there are many intellects (beings), there is a sense in which there is but one Intellect (being, substance) is widespread in the *Enneads*. One of the clearest and most extensive presentations is VI.2.20. There, as here (44–45), he uses science and branches of science as an illustration or analogy of the relationship between the single comprehensive item and the more specific ones. On this analogy see Commentary 4.2 and Introduction, Section 2. On the intelligibles and souls as "unlimited" (*apeiroi*) see next chapter, 4.5, 1–11 and Commentary.

Chapter 5

The soul constantly gives to extension but is not reduced thereby.

5, 1–11 *The greatness of . . . able to bear*: This chapter is about "the size of the soul." This is an expansion on a theme Plotinus has already made some remarks about in 2, 25–34, where he claimed that it is a mistake to think of the soul as small and the extension of body as large: it is actually the body that is small and the soul that is large. As Tornau notes *ad loc.*, here this theme is prompted by the remark at the end of the previous chapter that the Soul is unlimited. Plotinus begins by saying that the largeness of soul is to be understood in the same way, i.e., not as greatness in volume. Just as the soul is unlimited in the sense of having no exclusive internal boundaries, it is unlimited in being an inexhaustible source. Thus, the first 11 lines of the chapter expound the idea of undiminished giving: the soul constantly gives to extension but is not reduced thereby. This idea of undiminished giving pervades Plotinus' metaphysics: it holds for procession from the first principle, the One, and for Intellect and Soul, cf. Introduction, Section 5. For its Platonic sources, see Emilsson (2007, ch. I, sec. 7).

The question "For how could it be absent . . . ?" in 5 is a citation from Plato's *Parmenides* 144b3–5. As Tornau notes, the "ever-flowing nature," which is not yet in flux (5–6), is a quote from the famous Pythagorean oath by the *tetraktus*, which is the number 10, the sum of the first four numbers, found in the Pythagorean *Golden Verses*, 47. The words in 10–11 "as this universe is able to bear" allude again to the doctrine of reception according to the capacity of the recipient. (See Commentary 4.3, 6–12 and Introduction, Section 3.)

5, 11–22 *We should not . . . soul as well*: In this latter half of the chapter, Plotinus warns against any comparison of the respective quantities of the soul and the body of the universe: the fact that the soul is without size does not mean that it is "very small" compared with its body. The terms "large" and "small" do not apply to it at all in the quantitative sense they apply to body. The point made in 18–22 that the fact that the soul expands as the body grows is evidence of the greatness of soul does not mean that the soul can become so and so many cubic meters larger but that there is endless supply for it to animate whatever quantity.

Chapter 6

If souls can animate any quantity, why does not each animate the whole? How come that not every soul is aware of whatever any other is aware of?

6, 1–5 *Why then does . . . added to them*: The question raised in the first line of this chapter arises in direct continuation of the end of the previous chapter: if the soul can ensoul an ever larger volume as the body grows, why doesn't it go beyond the boundaries of its body and ensoul a different one? The theme of the lack of boundary between souls at the end of Chapter 4 as well as the whole discussion of the unity of soul in that chapter also makes this question a natural one to ask. The answers Plotinus gives to it here are highly elliptical and partly difficult to interpret. Plotinus' immediate and brief answer in 1–3 is: a given soul does not go beyond the boundaries of its body to ensoul a different body because that other body is already ensouled. This answer, however, turns out to be superficial and unsatisfactory because a deeper question immediately presents itself: in virtue of what can we maintain that the soul occupying the other body is a different one from the one occupying the body we started out from? In other words: what individuates souls (3–4)?

Plotinus affirms that the souls "differ as well in what is added to them" (4–5). This sentence leaves, of course, a lot to be desired in terms of lucidity. What are these additions to the souls? As Tornau *ad loc.* suggests, it presumably is the different organic bodies: each soul is set over a particular body, which could be described as an addition to it during the embodiment. This, however, does of course not mean that the soul becomes in any way corporeal, i.e., the body is not added as an element of the soul itself. Most translators leave untranslated what corresponds to "as well" (*kai*) in our translation. We think that it makes reasonably good sense to see here an allusion to the difference between souls prior to embodiment stated in 4, 38ff. So the souls are said to differ with respect to what is added to these prior differences. Tornau *ad loc.* mentions this as a possibility but does not wholeheartedly endorse it.

One may wonder why Plotinus does not make use of the plurality of souls at the intelligible level asserted in Chapter 4 in order to account for the individuality of the embodied souls. The answer is presumably that the former individuality, whatever it exactly amounts to, would not be of much help to tackle the questions that occupy him here. In 4, 43ff. we see that souls are "present to one another without becoming alien to one another" and "not marked off from one another by boundaries." So the souls at this level presumably share each other's knowledge and have no absolute boundaries. The embodied souls, by contrast, apparently do not share each others' consciousness and have clear boundaries.

6, 5–13 *Then how is . . . in our head*: With the last sentence in 4–5 about the additions to the souls the text becomes extremely elliptical and difficult to grasp. It will stay so throughout the chapter. The following is the best we can make of it.

Given that the additions that differentiate the souls are the different bodies, the question in 5–7 naturally arises: why is the same soul in the hand and in the foot while the soul in this part of the universe is different from that in that one? Arguably, on Plotinian principles, the soul in the hand and the soul in the foot ensoul different bodies— different bodily parts are different extended items (cf. 4.1, 15–24). It makes a difference, however, whether the bodies are continuous: in IV.9.2, 11–12 it is suggested that if you and me were to share sense-perceptions, our bodies would have to be continuous. By this Plotinus presumably has in mind that our bodies would have to be organically continuous, not merely constituting one solid bulk. Each human and animal body is organically continuous in this way but neither the large body of the universe nor yours and mine (which are, actually, parts of that of the universe) are organically continuous in this way.

In 7–8 we have: "If the perceptions are different, then we should note that the accompanying affections are different as well." As Tornau notes, this is presumably an elliptical sentence meaning roughly: if someone should point out that the perceptions in the different parts of the universe, i.e., the perceptions of different organisms, are different, i.e., not shared, then we should note that different affections must be underlying this difference in the sense-perceptions. This sentence and the sequel suggest that Plotinus wishes to put much of the responsibility for different perceptions in different subjects on differences in their bodies and their affections. A very brief summary of Plotinus' views on the body, affections, and sense-perception is therefore in order.

The body that is subject to the sort of affections at issue here is not just any kind of body but a qualified body (*toionde sōma*, cf. Aristotle, *On the Soul* [*De Anima*] II.1, 412a21; 412b15). This is a body that has a trace (*ichnos, indalma*) of soul (cf. in addition to 4.15, 13–17 below:

IV.4.18, 1–9 and 29–34; 27, 1–13; 28, 1–21 and 52–76, 29.1–7 and 50–5). This "trace of soul" is not an entity of the order of soul but a kind of immanent hylomorphic form: Igal (1979), Tornau ad 4.15, 15, and Noble (2013). It differs, however, from mere bodily qualities in that it endows the body with features signifying life: ability to sustain itself, react to the environment in ways a mere body is incapable of and the like. The affections (path) involved in sense-perception or physical pleasure and pain have the living body with its trace of soul as subject: a mere, lifeless body is incapable of having these kinds of affections (IV.4.18, 7–9). Sense-perceptions are, however, more than mere affections of the sense-organs, even if these affections are of a special kind. Strictly speaking sense-perception is a judgment (*krisis*) based on or from the sensory affection; it is an act of the individual soul, not of the body or the trace of soul. Cf. III.6.1, 1ff.; IV.4.23; see also Emilsson (1988), especially chapters IV and VII. For a somewhat different view on sense-perception in Plotinus see Smith (2006) and Magrin (2010), and also Chiaradonna (2012).

What follows in 8–13 is very cryptic. Clearly, however, a comparison between the soul in different parts of an individual and different souls is being made. Clearly, also, the discussion proceeds from the assumption that the sense in which all souls are but one soul is the same or at least analogous to the sense in which there is just soul animating each one of us even in different bodily parts.

In 8–11 Plotinus is talking about different individual souls, saying that that in them which judges is the same, whereas the bodily affections differ. A strange claim indeed, which he does not sustain to the end, at least not consistently. In 11–13 he compares this case of different individual souls with the case within a human being: here the same judge judges the affections of the head and the toe. This interpretation requires the slight emendation suggested by Kirchhoff of adding "the" (*ho*) in front of "same" (*autos*) in 11. We find it better than the alternatives given by HS₂ and Tornau, which indeed keep the preserved text but yield, in our view, an unnatural sentence and less good meaning.

6, 13–20 *So why is . . . been discussed elsewhere*: The question in 13–14 as to why, if the case of different souls is similar to that of the individual in this way, one soul is not aware of the judgment of another, is to be expected: it would seem that the same in us judges the different affections. At this point Plotinus makes an unexpected move: within us are different sense-powers such as seeing and hearing, whose role he takes to be analogous to that of the different souls; they are not aware of each other's judgments (15–17); what is aware of the judgments of both sight and hearing is reason (*logismos*), which is different from and presumably set over both (17). This opens the possibility that on the cosmic scale there is something, the hypostasis Soul, perhaps, which is aware of the doings of the individual souls even if they are not aware of this or of each other's doings.

This account may be internally consistent but it is worrisome for several reasons. One reason is that elsewhere, notably in IV.2.2 and IV.7, 6–7, Plotinus argues from the unity of consciousness of the perceptive soul (not reason) in different organs and parts of the body for the presence of the numerically same soul in the different parts. The argumentative strategy of these passages even suggests that if the situation is like what is insinuated here in our passage, namely that, e.g., sight is unaware of what hearing is judging, we should conclude that sight and hearing are different souls and that there is no unity of the individual soul. For the unity of perception in Plotinus see Emilsson (1988, ch. V).

Secondly, there is an element in Plotinus' account here not addressed so far: the relevance of the difference between judgment and affection. His last probing question—and answer—about this matter is: "So why is the one soul not aware of the other soul's judgment?—Precisely because it is a judgment, and not an affection" (13–15). This is not a very satisfactory argument. First, reason is supposedly able to share in another's judgment without difficulty. So why should not another judging power be able to do so? No explanation is given of this. Perhaps the underlying reasoning here is as follows: different souls are attached to different bodies, which are the subjects of different affections. Each soul only judges the affections it is organically in contact with and other souls need not be aware of that at all, even if they may (cf. 18–20). Similarly, within the same individual soul a given sense judges only the affections it is set over and in contact with. If, on the other hand, my soul had shared in the affection in your body, I would indeed have been aware of it. This may be reasonable in its own right but it does not answer the question why two sense-powers of one and the same soul are not aware of each other's judgments. That question is pressing because much of Plotinus' account of sense-perception elsewhere points in a different direction.

The last sentence in 19–20, "this has been discussed elsewhere," undoubtedly refers to IV.9.2–3.

Chapter 7

Omnipresence of the selfsame soul illustrated with analogies from the sensible sphere.

There are no great philosophical novelties in this chapter. Plotinus' concern is not so much to develop his view. He is rather trying to render it credible and intuitive that even if his arguments have the force of necessity they fail to carry conviction, cf. the remark in 4, 5–6. He is trying to do something about that by taking analogies from the sensible world, manipulating them, and then presenting them as illustrations of the case of the soul.

7, 1–9 *But let us . . . what it controls*: In these lines Plotinus resumes here once again his main contentions in previous chapters and in our treatise generally: that "the same thing extends over everything." He clearly intends "the same" here to be understood as "strictly and numerically the same" as he does in previous chapters. This is of course his answer to the Sailcloth Dilemma in Plato's *Parmenides* 131b3–c8. Though none of the central terms of the previous discussion—soul, the whole, being or intellect—are explicitly mentioned in this chapter, the focus makes it quite clear that it is soul he is concerned with: he is concerned with an intelligible's presence to the sensible and the sole intelligible being that can be said to be so present is soul. The key idea in 3–9 that the many come to and are united in one thing that is not divided over the many is first expressed in Chapter 3.

7, 9–22 *Yet a hand . . . yet be undivided*: In these lines we have an analogy of a hand holding out a long plank. Plotinus' claim is that the power of the hand is present as a whole to every part of the plank; it is not the case, in other words, that some of the power is in this part and some in that other. So this is supposed to give us something familiar which is similar to the undivided presence of the soul in bodies. In 18–20 he manipulates the example by proposing that we remove in our thought the mass of the hand and leave the power intact. The claim is that in that case we would have to concede that the power would be one and the same undivided everywhere in the plank.

The argument in 12–15, " . . . the power, . . . controlling." may appear somewhat obscure. The main point seems to be that the extension of the power has nothing to do with the size of the hand. Tornau *ad loc.* may be right in suggesting that the qualifying "it seems" has the function of suggesting that actually the power is not limited by the size of the plank either; its being so limited is a mere appearance disproved by the case of an extension of the plank developed in the following lines.

7, 22–39 *Indeed, if you . . . the spherical body*: In these lines Plotinus develops a new image: Think of a sphere with a transparent surface and a small luminous body inside it. He believes this example illustrates the same point as the previous one of the hand holding a staff and more or less in the same way: the same light coming from a light source, he claims, is everywhere in the outer luminous body just like the same power, coming from the hand, extends to the whole staff. Again, he asks us to think away the corporeal aspect of the source, i.e., the little luminous body, which in any case did not possess the light "*as* body" (31). Then we would have to admit that the same light was present everywhere in the outer sphere.

Some further general comments on this are in order. As noted by Schroeder (1992, 24), Plotinus' two analogies can be seen in the context of the Sailcloth Dilemma in Plato's *Parmenides* 131b3–c8. Socrates first suggests that the one Form is like the day, which is undivided in many places at once. Parmenides reinterprets this as meaning that it is like one sailcloth over many persons. This gets Socrates into trouble as he is forced to admit that different parts of the sail cover different persons; if the Form and the particulars are like that, particulars do not participate in one and the same thing but each in different parts. Socrates might have fared better if he had stuck to his analogy of the day. At any rate, we can see Plotinus' analogies of the hand and the luminous body as attempts at providing examples from the familiar sensible realm that exhibit undivided presence to many sensible particulars. One can even see his example of the luminous body as a development of the Day Analogy in the *Parmenides* 131b3–6, even if Plotinus admittedly could have thought of independent reasons for focusing on light. A crucial difference between the sailcloth, on the one hand, and the power of the hand and the light, on the other, is that Plotinus' examples, even if they are of perfectly familiar sensible phenomena, involve incorporeal phenomena, viz., the power and the light.

From the viewpoint of modern physics, Plotinus' two examples may not warrant the conclusion that something is one and the same undivided in many. If we consider especially the case of the luminous body, however, we may note that what Plotinus says here is quite in harmony with his general views on light: ordinary light is the external activity, a kind of by-product of the internal activity of an original source of light such as a fire. The external activity depends on the internal one and is a weaker

expression of it. This is what external light is according
to Plotinus: it is not a quality of bodies but an incorporeal
activity (cf. 31–33). Apparently, it is instantaneous. For
Plotinus' fullest discussion of light, see IV.5, 7–8; for
further discussion, see Schroeder (1992, ch. 2), and
Tornau *ad loc.* For the role of light and light metaphors in
Plotinus' metaphysics, see Schroeder (1992). For the role
of internal and external activity in Plotinus and further
references, see Introduction, Section 5.

7, 39–47 *Moreover, in the . . . any particular place*: Here
Plotinus makes more or less the same point with respect
to the light of the sun: it is only because the sun is a
luminous body that we see whence the light comes. In
42–44 he makes the point that the light is undivided
everywhere and that this is shown by the fact that when
the light is cut off by an object it is prevented from being
on the opposite side to that facing the source (cf. also
Marcus Aurelius 8.57 and 12.30). Why would one think
that this showed the *undivided* presence of the light?
Presumably because if the light really were divided, there
should still be some on the side that, as a matter of fact,
is immediately darkened; this shows, Plotinus claims, that
there was not one piece of the light here, and another
there.

Chapter 8

The conclusions of the previous chapter applied to purely immaterial beings to whom spatial divisibility is even less applicable than to physical powers and light.

In this chapter the conclusions and indications of the previous chapter are generalized: that which is not only incorporeal but also immaterial cannot be divided and must be participated in as a whole. Much of what is said is familiar from previous chapters. A few additional points, however, emerge.

8, 1–8 *In the case . . . and another there*: There is a transition here from the topic of light, which even if itself bodiless (*asōmatos*) nevertheless needs a body, to something immaterial (*ahylos*), which can exist independently of matter and bodies. Plotinus has not used the expression "immaterial" before in the treatise. The meaning is "without sensible matter." As Tornau notes, the contrasting term is "in matter" (*enylos*). Bodies are the primary items "in matter" in Plotinus' ontology but also features bound up with bodies such as so-called "forms in matter" (cf. Commentary 4.1, 15–24). Thus, "immaterial" is not quite the same as "bodiless" or "incorporeal" (*asōmatos*). The claim is clearly that if what has been said of light and a corporeally bound power such as that of the hand holds, then all the more it should hold of something immaterial, i.e., something that can exist without sensible matter.

8, 9–12 *So we can . . . by being divided*: Participation has only been mentioned once so far in the treatise (2, 18). Hitherto Plotinus has made more use of expressions such as "present to it as a whole" or "being undivided as a whole in the many." Participation, which for Plotinus is roughly equivalent to the previous expressions (see, however, Commentary 4.3, 6–12) now becomes central in the account: he describes the soul-body relationship in terms of the body's participation in soul. This is a sign of the fact discussed in the Introduction, Section 6, that Plotinus takes the puzzles about participation in Plato's *Parmenides* primarily to apply to soul. That is also why he connects them with the interpretation of the *Timaeus* 35a, in particular of the problematic phrase that the soul becomes divisible about bodies, which Plotinus does not accept at face value (see Commentary 4.1, 2).

8, 12–15 *For being affected . . . of a body*: Only items with body can be affected. We noted in connection with 4.5, 1–11 Plotinus' doctrine of "undiminished giving," i.e., that the intelligible causes are in no way reduced by proceeding and making something lesser than themselves. He holds quite generally that the causes are not affected, changed, at all as a result of their causal activity. Only bodies can be affected. Plotinus wrote a whole treatise, *Ennead* III.6, to which Porphyry gave the title "On the impassibility of things without body," defending this view.

8, 17–19 *Indeed it is . . . will be indivisible.* Being divisible or divided in the sense of having distinct spatial parts that have no community between them is the essential characteristic of bodies (cf. 4.1, 22–23). To be divided or divisible implies that something can happen to or characterize a part without applying to the whole. It is this sort of spatial divisibility that Plotinus so strongly wants to deny for soul in our treatise: it cannot be divided into distinct, independent parts along with the distinct parts of the body that it ensouls.

8, 22–28 *Thus whenever you . . . depart from itself:* The word "it" in 23 and preceding lines refers to "a thing that belongs to no body" in 15. These lines pick up and partly repeat material from 4.3, 12–19. Plotinus does not deny that that there is a sense in which this "thing that belongs to no body" is in the many bodies inasmuch as it acts in them, but it does not belong to any of them (cf. Tornau *ad loc.*). The way he speaks of "in many" and "in them" in 22 and 25, respectively, suggests that he may have in mind Plato's *Parmenides* 131b3–c8. The phrase "not departing from itself" is from Plato's *Phaedrus* 245c (cf. also *Parmenides* 144c). Plotinus commonly uses it to indicate the self-containment of his principles, which is an essential aspect of his double act doctrine (cf. Introduction, Section 5). Common equivalent expressions are "remaining" and "together with itself."

8, 28–36 *Nor is it . . . of being divided*: That size, in the concrete sense in which corporeal items have size, does not apply to non-bodily entities is already suggested in 4.2, 25–34 and commonly elsewhere. When Plotinus says in 32 that not *even* qualities belong to what has no body (this involves an emendation in harmony with Ficino's reading adopted by Creuzer and HS₂), the underlying thought is presumably that qualities are somewhat closer to the intelligible than quantities. As noted above (Commentary 1, 15–24), the defining characteristic of bodies is spatial quantity or size. In IV.2.1, 29ff. and here in Chapter 1, it seems that qualities come on top of this corporeal nature: they may be the same in form in many but this form becomes individuated according to the underlying bodily bulk (cf. Commentary 1, 15–24). Elsewhere Plotinus indeed holds that both qualities and quantities are somehow present in the transcendent intelligible realm (see, e.g., VI.2.13 and 14). This, however, does not mean that the qualities and quantities exist as such in that realm: the point is that there is something in the intelligible realm corresponding to the quantities and qualities in the sensible realm from which the latter are derived.

8, 37–45 *Therefore it must . . . are not striving*: These lines resume thoughts already present in Chapter 2. Given Plotinus' general scheme, every "downward" movement is accompanied by a converse, "epistrophic," movement toward the source. These latter movements are usually described in psychological terms of desiring, longing or, as here, striving (*ephesis*). So, the many strive for one thing, not different parts of that one thing. They receive that one thing not in such a way that it or anything of it becomes the private property of each, but each partakes of the whole. For this notion of striving or desiring one's source, see Commentary 2, 34–49.

Chapter 9

Several varieties of a hypothesis, according to which what comes to be in the many is cut off from its source, are considered and rejected.

This chapter continues the preceding one directly, but there is a change of focus. Plotinus here considers several varieties of a hypothesis according to which what comes to be in the many, the immanent thing, is cut off from its source. Bréhier (1936, 165–166) suggested that this chapter is an interpretation of Plato's *Parmenides* 142b1–144c2. This is a part of the second hypothesis of the *Parmenides*, which according to Plotinus describes the sphere of Intellect and being (Platonic Ideas). As we have seen, the problem Plotinus is tackling can be traced back to the dilemmas of *Parmenides* 131a4–e3, which seem to question the undivided presence of the Idea in many particulars. In 144b1–e7 it is argued that being and unity have infinite parts (at least as many as the numbers). At face value this speaks against everything that Plotinus has been maintaining inasmuch as it is asserted here that there are "parts" of being. So Plotinus sets out interpreting the passage, starting from a quite literal interpretation and ending with a much freer one that takes "parts" in the sense of "powers."

With the suggestion that the parts are powers of a transcendent entity Plotinus' double act doctrine becomes relevant and is brought to bear on the discussion, for powers in such a context are equivalent to external acts. A crucial aspect of this doctrine is the claim that an external act is not cut off from the internal one. For Plotinus' views on internal and external activity and the concomitant notion of "not being cut off from" see Introduction, Section 5. We take it that embodied souls are still the case of immanence that he is concerned with even if he does not use the word "soul." The whole discussion here is still an attempt to deal with the Sailcloth Dilemma. The interpretation given here is basically the same as Tornau's.

9, 1–7 *For if the . . . which they derive*: Plotinus first considers a version of the hypothesis that what comes to be in each of the many, i.e., presumably, in each ensouled being, is a part of the "primary item" (the hypostasis Soul or perhaps being); each such part is, according to the hypothesis, a whole and like the original primary item but cut off from it. This hypothesis is rejected for two reasons: (1) Each of these parts would then be primary like the original primary item, and, hence—this seems to be the implicit conclusion—the hypothesis makes nonsense of the distinction between primary and secondary items. (2) Nothing seems to prevent these parts from constituting one and the same thing: they do not come to belong to their respective bodies and are not there made different from each other by virtue of the bodies. Hence—this is again merely implicit—the hypothesis that presumed that there were different parts fails to make good sense of how they differ; they, in fact, seem to coalesce into one item which is just a replica of the original item.

9, 7–25 *But if these . . . greater than substance*: Here Plotinus modifies his interpretation: what if these so-called parts are powers? The hypothesis is still that these parts (powers) are cut off from the primary item. The shift to powers at least indicates that what now is supposed to come to be present in each is something subordinate to the primary item. The hypothesis now is close to a suggestion that was addressed and rejected in Chapter 4, 7–18: the whole (being) sends off powers and that it is these rather than the whole itself that is immediately present in the sensible. This suggestion receives a much longer and fuller treatment and refutation in the present chapter than it did in Chapter 4. Plotinus proceeds to raise several critical questions about it. The hypothesis conflicts with some basic tenets of his metaphysics such as that of undiminished giving (see Commentary 4.5, 1–11) or the indivisible unity of the transcendent realm (see Commentary 4.2).

9, 7–9 *But if these . . . longer be whole.* The thought is presumably that every intelligible power contains all, but what is activated depends on the capacity of the recipient. For this doctrine, see Introduction, Section 3. If this is not the supposition and the powers indeed are whole, the hypothesis is really no different from the previous one according to which the powers are wholes.

9, 9–11 *Next, how could . . . point while proceeding*: This is a very elliptical argument. Presumably, the sense is: if the subordinate powers are cut off from their source, they will have left it behind at some point; but if so, how are we going to explain that they have arrived at the many? How have they managed to proceed any further after they were cut off from their source?

9, 11–16 *Also, are the . . . their own substances*: If the powers that are cut off from their source in this way no longer exist in the source, the source has been diminished. This, however, conflicts with the basic principle of undiminished giving (see Commentary 4.5, 1–11).

9, 16–25 *If they are . . . greater than substance*: In these lines Plotinus brings up various possibilities of a positive elucidation of the supposition in 16, "If they exist both in the source and elsewhere, . . . ," all of which he, however, rejects. The supposition is still that the parts (powers) are cut off from their sources. In some cases the possibilities he considers split up into alternatives only some of which are pursued. The result is a quite complex and again elliptical train of reasoning. The following is what we make of it:

Suppose A: The parts, or powers, exist both in their sources and in the many (16).

Then either (A1) they exist as wholes in the many (16–17), or (A2) they exist as parts in the many (17).

If A2, then (A2.1) what remains in the source will be parts (17–18). Presumably the idea is that if the power is split so that one part is in the source and another in the sensible realm, the power is no longer whole in the source. We must bear in mind that the argument proceeds on the hypothesis that the immanent powers are cut off from their sources. If so, the source has been diminished and we have again the same unacceptable situation as before.

If A1, then either (A1.1) the powers are the same and undivided in the many as in the source (18–20) or (A1.2) the powers are many and each a whole and similar to the others (20–21).

A1.1 asserts the paradoxical conclusion that Plotinus is willing to embrace, viz., that the same is undividedly present in many. The hypothesis under consideration, however, seeks to avoid this conclusion with the aid of the notion of a power as an intermediary between the intelligible source and the sensibles. The present alternative only makes the problem recur with respect to the immanent powers (cf. Tornau *ad loc.*). The sense in which "each is a whole" in A1.2 is "not split into a part remaining in the source and a part present in the sensible." Thus, again as Tornau *ad loc.* notes, the sense of "whole" here is different from the sense in 16 and 18, where "whole" refers to the totality of powers.

If A1.2, then (A1.2.1): each power will be with its substance (21) or (A1.2.2) one power only is with its substance, the rest are mere powers without their substance (22–23). A1.2.1 has the multiplication of the substances as a consequence. For many powers in the many sensibles, each tied to its substance, will require as many separate substances. But this conflicts with the unity of being.

A1.2.2: Suppose one power is attached to its substance, the others separate. This saves the hypothesis from positing many distinct substances. As Tornau notes *ad loc.*, even though A1.2.2 sounds like a mere abstract possibility, in the context of Plotinus' worldview it could be given a concrete sense by supposing that the one power to be attached to its substance is the World-Soul, whereas the other powers would be the other individual souls which are taken to be separated from their substance. This, however, would leave some powers unattached, cut off from their source, which would be an unacceptable conclusion (23–24).

9, 25–35 *But if the . . . lack of power*: In these lines Plotinus introduces a new conception: the powers derived from the primary item are a weaker version of the latter like a weak light going out from a bright one. If this is so, the powers must be the same in kind, i.e., at least specifically identical (30). This would follow from the fact that each depends on the same substance or being. Given this there are two possibilities: either the powers are numerically identical so that the very same power is everywhere or at least, in case there is merely specific identity, the same power is present as a whole everywhere in the body it operates in. If this is not so and the power is parceled over the body, the power will be infinitely divided along with the body, which is incompatible with their being powers: in this case they would have been reduced to something belonging to the body and suffer the same sort of divisibility as it.

9, 36 *Secondly, the fact . . . there being consciousness*: The point here is presumably that if the same power is not present everywhere or the different powers do not unite in a single power, there will be no unity of consciousness, i.e., no single subject which is aware of differently located sensations (cf. 4.1, 24–29 and Commentary).

9, 37–45 *Further, just as . . . without being divided*: Plotinus is here envisaging that the relationship between the source and what comes to be in the many is a case of internal vs. external activity or, which is really the same thing, a prototype and its image (see Introduction, Section 5).

Chapter 10

Objections from the examples of portraits and heat to the claim of constant dependence of image on archetype considered and rejected.

10, 1–5 *But if someone. . . fire is gone*: This chapter directly continues the end of Chapter 9. The reflection (*indalma*) spoken of there (4.9, 37) is the same thing as the image (*eidōlon*) in 4.10, 1. Plotinus here discusses objections to his statement in 4.9, 37–39 that an image cannot exist cut off from its source. The objector points out that a likeness (*eikôn*) such as a portrait exists in the absence of the original (*archetypos*) and that things can be hot in the absence of fire. Plotinus responds to these in turn.

10, 5–17 *In the first . . . from their priors*: As to the former objection, Plotinus notes that neither the original nor the painter produces the painting by itself. As Tornau notes *ad loc.*, in artificial production of images such as painting, the formal cause and the efficient cause fall apart: the painter is needed to bring about the image, whereas the model determines its features. Even in the case where the painter makes a self-portrait, a distinction is to be made between his body as model and him as the artist: it is not as a colored bodily figure that the painter accomplishes the painting (8–11). Image-making in the strict sense occurs when there is coincidence of the formal and efficient cause and the image constantly depends on the cause as is the case with reflections in water, mirrors, and shadows.

10, 17–30 *As for what . . . argued extensively elsewhere*: Against the objection concerning heat that heat remains in the absence of fire, Plotinus advances three arguments.

In 18–20 he claims that heat should not be called a likeness of fire, unless it is presumed that there is some fire in the heat. But if so, the likeness, heat, is there only so long as there is fire present and the remaining heat is not rightly called a likeness of fire. So, the argument claims, in so far as the heat is rightly called likeness of fire, there is no separation of the maker (fire) and the likeness (heat). This argument may look suspect as it stands. Plotinus may, however, be presuming a distinction between heat as the external activity of a living fire and heat as a mere quality of the bodies that have been made hot (cf. Tornau *ad loc.*). Thus, his counter-argument states that only the former kind of heat is rightly called likeness. This distinction parallels the distinction between soul and its activities, and the trace of soul that constitutes the qualified body: this trace is not soul in its own right but a product of soul pertaining to the body. Like the heat of warmed animal bodies, it can linger for a while in the absence of the soul itself (cf. IV.4.29, 1–9; for the trace of soul see Commentary 4.6, 5–13). If this is indeed what Plotinus has in mind, his argument is extremely elliptical.

In Plotinus' second counter-argument (20–24) to the point that things can be hot in the absence of fire clearly assumes that the heat in question is the bodily quality, which according to the interpretation given of the previous argument does not count as a likeness of fire. He points out that such heat gradually vanishes in the absence of fire (20–22), i.e., when cut off from the source. If the relationship between the intelligible source and its powers is like that, there would be only one imperishable thing. The idea is presumably that everything except the first principle, for Plotinus the One or the Good, is in a sense a power of that first principle. That is indeed a statement Plotinus could subscribe to. The present hypothesis, however, goes further than that: the powers of this first cause are cut off from it and, hence, are perishable like the heat of the stone. If that were so, soul and Intellect would be perishable, which is, of course, an unacceptable conclusion.

The third counter-argument (24–30), which is a close sequel to the second, claims that the objection implies that invariable causes may have effects that are in flux. This is, however, not even the case in the sensible world, responds Plotinus: if the sun stayed in the same place, it would give the same light to the same places. Why does Plotinus suppose that the original objection that an effect can exist in the absence of the source implies that invariable causes can have variable effects? It is not clear at all how this should follow. Presumably Plotinus is here not so much objecting to the supposition that an image (effect) can exist in the absence of its archetype (cause) as to the supposition that the kind of invariable causes he is presuming can be in flux. In other words, he is denying that they can be absent, which is a premise of the objection.

The reference of "its" in 29 is no doubt to the first principle, the One (the Good), which is alluded to in 23. Intellect and Soul are what derives from the One. The reference to earlier work in 30 can be, e.g., IV.7; VI.9.9; and V.1.6.

Chapter 11

If the intelligible is undividedly present to many, how are differences between the many to be explained?

This chapter raises two questions initially: given the main thesis of undivided presence in many, (1) why does not everything participate in the intelligible as a whole and (2) why are there differences of rank within the intelligible realm?

11, 3–9 *We must think . . . what is turbid*: The answer to (1) is the doctrine of reception according to the capacity of the recipient, for which see the Introduction, Section 3. So, even physical recipients differ in their capacities to receive, and this explains why not everything participates in everything.

"The transparent" (*to diaphanes*) in 8 is the medium of light in Aristotle's theory of light (cf. *On the Soul* [*De Anima*] 418b4ff.). Plotinus does not normally appeal to this theory in his accounts of light and vision, for which see IV.5. The "differentiae" in 10 are the Aristotelian differentiae, which differentiate between kinds of things: rationality, for instance, is what differentiates human beings among animals.

11, 9–25 *And the primary . . . way than these*: These lines address (2) above. One may wonder why undivided presence prompts the second question, because undivided presence has in the preceding chapters primarily been understood in terms of the intelligibles' relation to bodies, not the internal relations between intelligibles. Here, however, Plotinus takes this to refer to the latter as well, and this leads him to resume the account of Chapter 4, where the unity in diversity of the intelligible realm is discussed. Of course, undivided presence holds for the intelligibles internally as well as for sensibles, even if in the former case there can be no question of an undivided presence to different spatial locations. The account here is similar to the previous one in Chapter 4. Plotinus' dependence on the five greatest kinds of Plato's *Sophist* for accounting for the unity-in-plurality that characterizes the intelligible world is, however, more marked here in that the Form otherness, which in Plato is one of the Forms that share in being, is clearly affirmed as one of the intelligibles.

11, 9–10 *And the primary . . . of their locations*: The phrase "the primary, secondary and tertiary items" is based on

Plato's 2nd Letter, 312e 3–5. For a fuller exegesis of this passage by Plotinus see VI.7.42.

11, 10–11 *For nothing prevents . . . greater and lesser*: On Plotinus' use of the co-presence of the branches of knowledge or the theorems of a science in a soul or mind to illustrate, even justify, his claims about intelligible unity in diversity, see Commentary 4.2.

11, 12–14 *For it is . . . from one another*: Many commentators, starting with Ficino, have remarked that the comparison with a complex sense-experience in 12–14 describes an experience of something like an apple: seeing it, tasting it, touching it, even hearing it as one sets one's teeth in it. Many translators and commentators take the phrase "from the same" as meaning "from the same object," as we do here. Tornau *ad loc.*, in the company of, e.g., HS₂, Bréhier, and Cilento, argues against this, preferring that "the same" refer to the totality of the experience. The way this is phrased, however, "*from* the same," without any evident allusion to a perceiver, rather suggests the object itself, e.g., the apple. Plotinus' point may well be that since we can note such co-presence of qualities even in sensible objects it should then not come as a surprise that we find this among intelligibles. The other interpretation is, however, fully possible.

11, 15–21 *Is it [being]. . . also existing separately*: That being (the intelligible realm) is at once unitary and variegated, one-many, is a commonplace in Plotinus (see Commentary 4.4).

In 16 Plotinus describes being as "a single yet variegated rational formula (*logos*)." The word *logos* already has a number of meanings and shades of meaning by Plato. When we come to Plotinus' times its uses are even more complex because it has been a key term in most of the philosophical schools in the intervening centuries. What will be said here only relates to *logos* as applied to the Plotinian system from the One "downward." This use, which presumably is the most common use in Plotinus, shows Stoic influence. *Logos* appears at every level of the Plotinian hierarchy except the top and the bottom, the One and matter. The general meaning seems to be "rationally arranged intelligible structure." Very often but not always and not here, *logos* is explicitly said to be the *logos* of something, e.g., soul is the *logos* of Intellect. In this usage that which the *logos* is a *logos* of is a higher, more unified, entity, which the *logos* expresses in a more explicit manner. On *logos* in Plotinus, see Gerson (2012).

That unity and being come hand in hand (16–17) is asserted in *Parmenides* 144b1–e7 and is a well-known tenet of Aristotle's (cf. *Metaphysics* 4.2.1003b22ff. and

7.16.1040b16ff.). In Plotinus the One, the first principle, is beyond being and substance, so the equivalence of being and unity holds primarily for the second hypostasis. The inference "if X is something determinate, then it is unitary" will, however, hold quite generally for Plotinus: to be something is to be something unified. Otherness is for Plotinus as for Plato (cf. *Sophist* 259a4–7) one of the Forms that *are,* i.e., partake in being. It is through otherness that the intelligible realm is diversified.

21–25 *But sensibles are . . . way than these*: Plotinus merely lists different modes of presence listed in these lines without explaining their differences. Presumably the presence of bodies to soul (23) exemplifies the presence of sensibles to intelligibles (21) and the presence of a science to science exemplifies the presence of intelligibles to intelligibles. It characterizes the latter relationship that a partial science contains the whole of which it is a part; it can be said to be this whole (cf. VI.2.20). The body that is present to soul, by contrast, can in no sense be said to be the soul.

Chapter 12

The presence of an utterance (logos) to many ears used to illustrate the presence of the same soul to many bodies.

This chapter picks up one of the modes of presence listed at the end of the previous chapter, namely body's presence to soul, which so far has been and will continue to be a primary concern in this treatise. Here Plotinus develops yet another set of analogies from the sensible sphere that are supposed to make the undivided presence to many understandable or at least in a way familiar. This time it is the way in which an utterance (*logos*) is present in the air between a speaker and many hearing ears. He also brings up to the same effect the presence of a form (*morphē*) in the air available to all present eyes to see. He claims that the utterance is present as a whole everywhere in the air. It is not the case that some part of the utterance is in this part of the air and another one in another part, as is proved by the fact that listeners standing apart all hear the utterance equally. So the so-called embodied souls correspond to the utterance heard by the different ears, the utterance as it exists in the speaker corresponds to the soul prior to embodiment.

12, 1–5 *Just as when . . . to the utterance*: We see here that Plotinus distinguishes between the voice (*phonē*) and the utterance (*logos*), the latter being the meaningful content of the former. The claim that the same is present everywhere is more feasible if it is taken to apply to the utterance, understood as meaningful content, than if it is taken to apply to the voice or sound as such. Presumably, it is the former that he intends.

12, 4–14 *And many eyes . . . all its participants*. Plotinus' main account of the transmission from object of vision to the eye is in IV.5.1–5. He makes the same point there as here that the form coming from the object is everywhere in the intermediate space (IV.5.3, 33–36). The accounts differ, however, in that here, in 10–11, he allows that the air may be affected by the form, a point he strongly argues against in IV.5.2–4. The remark in 12–13 that not every opinion would agree with what he has said is, however, not made to mark a deviation from his own view on visual transmission. The affection of the air is inessential to his main point here, which is the unity of the object seen by many. This view, which claims the presence of the same form everywhere in the air, is clearly inconsistent with other theories of visual transmission, e.g., the Stoic one.

In 7–9 he explicitly raises the comparison with the soul-body relation: the presence of the soul to the body is said to be similar to the presence of the voice or the visible form to many ears or eyes. The soul-body relationship has not explicitly been an issue since Chapter 6 (except for the brief mention at the end of Chapter 11). As we see it, this relationship is, however, what Plotinus has primarily in mind when talking about presence in the intervening chapters. The swift return to the topic of the soul-body relation, without introduction or warning as here, supports this.

12, 14–28 *It is clearer . . . and produces it*: These lines focus on the analogy of the voice, which he claims to show his point more clearly than that of the visual form (14–15). Yet again (cf. Chapter 4.7) he makes the point that a familiar everyday phenomenon exhibits the feature of undivided omnipresence that is so hard to believe in so that it should not be so difficult to accept this for the case of the soul (18–23).

In 23–28 Plotinus expands his analogy: the voice in the air is also in the speaker, i.e., it has not as it were left the speaker behind: in speaking the speaker both produces the voice and has it in himself. The voice in the speaker is clearly meant to be analogous to the undescended soul or Intellect, the hearing ear corresponds to body that

participates in soul and the voice in the air to the soul
that the body reaches out to receive. It is, on Plotinus'
view, however, in every instance the same voice. Clearly,
Plotinus is attributing the features of double activity (cf.
Introduction, Section 5) to the voice story: the upshot is
that the voice in the air (or the ears) is not cut off from
that in the speaker.

12, 28–37 *The case of . . . into this realm*: In these lines
Plotinus continues to emphasize two points already
familiar from earlier chapters, Chapters 2–4, in particular:
in being present to body the soul does not cease to exist
by itself and whatever participates in the intelligible
realm participates in it as a whole. We see here lucid
presentations of these points but substantially there
is little new in relation to what has come earlier. The
reference of "the other nature" in 30 is to the intelligible
realm to which the soul belongs.

Plotinus makes a reservation that his analogies may not
be perfect, even if there is similarity between them and
the object of comparison (28–29). He does not explain
what is unsatisfactory with his analogies. The context
suggests, however, that despite the claim in 23 ff. that the
voice in the speaker and in the air is one and the same,
he still fears the analogy may indicate that some of the
soul is in body, some disembodied. So in what follows

he emphasizes that even when embodied the soul "exists whole in itself and only appears to be in many" (32). The reference of "the other nature" in 30 is to the intelligible realm to which the soul belongs.

He emphasizes here that the soul *appears* to be "in the many" (32) and *seems* "to have entered this world" (37). He clearly understands "being in the many" and having "entered this world" as incompatible with the soul being "by itself." This means that what the souls *appears* to be is something of the body and parceled over bodies, i.e., something whose being depends on the bodies they ensoul. This, however, is a mere appearance. That which "is said to 'have come forth'" in 36 is probably a reference to the myth of the *Phaedrus*, which describes the souls as descending into bodies (cf. 248e).

12, 38–50 *For indeed, how . . . divided, but whole*: In these lines Plotinus presents arguments to hammer in the undivided presence of the soul. First he argues that (1) the souls are by themselves even if they are present to bodies. The argument for this is not altogether lucid. One of the premises for this is that "it is now seen as present" (38). This is shown by the phenomena of life and is uncontroversial. The other premise is that the soul is present "not because it waited for something to participate in it" (39). This is obscure. What he may mean is that the soul's presence does not depend on something's participation. So the soul is there by itself quite independently of the bodies. Then, if (1), (2) the (ensouled) body has come to soul (40). If (2), body or whatever comes to soul comes to and participates in the whole of it, since it exists by itself and is not a volume (41–50).

The reference in 41 of "that which lies outside what exists in this manner" is bodily nature; that which in 42 "exists in this manner" is soul, i.e., that which exists by itself even if present to the many. By "cosmos of life" no doubt the realm of soul or even intelligible nature generally is intended (cf. Commentary 5.9.11–13).

Chapter 13

Sense-perception makes us think that the soul is extended; on the nature of participation.

13, 1–6 *How then does . . . it is unextended*: Once again Plotinus raises the question how the soul can extend throughout the universe (cf. 4.1, 8–9 and Commentary). He has in the previous chapters repeatedly insisted that it (or what comes to be present to the many) really is not extended itself. We should presumably understand the question at the beginning of the chapter here as a question about why the soul *seems* to be extended or why we tend to believe that it is, even if reason tells that it is not. The answer given to this question is that sense-perception makes us think so. Why would this be so? Surely the soul is not an object of sense-perception. That is true, but through sense-perception we are aware of extension, and we see signs of life in its different spatial parts; hence, we come to think that the soul which is responsible for this life is extended. As a matter of fact though, it is the whole of extension that participates in the unextended soul.

13, 6–14 *So if something . . . will become three*: Plotinus then embarks on an elucidation of the notion of participation. Participation is to provide an explanation of why something has a certain feature: X's participation in F accounts for why X comes to be F-like. It follows from this that nothing that by itself already is F-like participates in F. So body does not participate in body so as to become body, nor does size participate in size so as to become size. There emerges an understanding of participation according to which nothing participates in itself. This does not mean, however, that what is participated in does not itself have the feature that those participants receive by participation: it has that feature, not by participation, but by or of itself. Lines 12–14 allude to the discussion of the causality of the Ideas in *Phaedo* 101bff. For the notion of participation in our treatise, see Strange (1992).

13, 14–26 *Thus if what . . . whole of itself*: From the preceding considerations Plotinus concludes that if what is divided and extended participates in anything so as to acquire a certain feature, that in which it participates must be without extension. And if this is without extension, the argument continues, it must be without spatial properties altogether (14–18). He then reminds the readers that "without extension" is different from "very small" (19–21). Its lack of size does not even mean that it is an unextended point or a collection of an infinity of such points (22–24). The former would mean that the soul were present to only a point in the volume, the rest being soulless; the latter would render the presence of soul to a body discontinuous because there would always be soulless points between the ensouled points. From this Plotinus concludes that "if the whole extended body is going to possess it as a whole, it will have to possess it over the whole of itself" (24–26). This conclusion presumably means: if what extension participates in is partless and without spatial properties altogether, whatever part of extension participates in it must participate in it as whole and, hence, come to have it as a whole.

Chapter 14

The individual soul considered from an ethical and eschatological standpoint; the notion of the self.

This chapter and the two other remaining chapters of VI.4 focus on the individual soul from an ethical and eschatological standpoint. Plotinus raises two questions in 4.14, 1–2: "How does each person possess his own soul?" and "How is one soul good while the other is evil?" As he makes clear, both questions are prompted by the claim that all souls are one. For if this is so, the individuality of souls seems to become problematic. Likewise, the unity of soul may seem to make it difficult to maintain that one soul is good and another evil, by which he presumably means that one leads an honorable life, another a disgraceful life. He begins by giving a summary of the unity-in-multiplicity of the intelligible realm. Then he addresses the first question in 16ff. rephrasing it as the question "who are we?" The second question is first directly addressed in Chapter 15, 18ff. The myth of Plato's *Phaedrus*, 246a3–252c2, is very much in the background of Chapters 14 through 16.

14, 2–16 *It suffices also . . . depends upon it*: These lines
are yet another statement of the unity-in-plurality
characteristic of the intelligible realm (see Chapter 4
and Commentary). There are no substantial novelties
presented here concerning this issue. Plotinus reaffirms
that there are differences but without boundaries. The
role of this passage is presumably as a preliminary to
answering the first question. Clearly, however, this does
not address the issue of our individuality to which he
turns next.

"It" in 3 refers back to what is spoken of in 13, 14–15 as
"something of another kind," i.e., the intelligible entity
that is participated in. This is here said to be sufficient for
all the souls, because of its unlimitedness. On the senses
in which the intelligible can be said to be unlimited see
Commentary 4.5, 1–11. On "all things are together" in 4
see Commentary 4.4, 23–26 and Introduction.

14, 16 *But as for us—who are we?* Here Plotinus asks:
"Who are we?" He thereby introduces his usual term for
the self, *we*. As several studies confirm, Plotinus employs
the first person plural semi-technically to refer to the self,
to what each of us individually really is. As it turns out,
there are actually two kinds of self we find in Plotinus:
the so-called "empirical self" and the higher, intelligible
self. The former is mostly identified with our discursive

reason. This is where "we" mostly are, he says (I.1.7, 16–17), apparently meaning that discursive thought is what our conscious life mostly consists in. The intelligible self is the basis each person has in the intelligible world of which the empirical self is a descendant. These two selves are intimately connected: we might even say that the primary concern of Plotinus' philosophy is about raising the empirical self to the level of the intelligible self. In any case, here Plotinus emphasizes that there is an unbroken line to our higher selves, which, in turn, puts us into contact with the intelligible realm as a whole. For Plotinus' notion of the self see O'Daly (1973) and Remes (2007).

The reference to "what comes to be in time" in 17 points to the fact that the sensible world is in time and that the things in it are subject to change, generation, and destruction. The intelligible realm is free from all this. The phrase "before this becoming came to be" in 18 does not mean "prior to the generation of the world of becoming"—Plotinus believed it always existed—but rather something like "prior to our entering the realm of becoming," i.e., the realm of time, which we entered at our birth into the sensible realm. For a fuller discussion on Plotinus' views on time, see Commentary 5.11, 14–24.

14, 18–22 *Even before this . . . it even now*: Plotinus holds that prior to our embodiment each of us existed in the intelligible realm. That some of us were human beings then, others even gods, is an unusual remark. As Tornau notes *ad loc.*, Plotinus is generally more concerned with our present godliness through "assimilation to the divine" (see especially "On virtues" I.2) than our prior existence. It is in fact also asserted here that even now in our embodied state we are not cut off from this realm.

Does this passage assert the existence of Ideas or other intelligible counterparts of individuals? No, it neither asserts nor denies this. It merely asserts that there is something at the intelligible level from which each one of us is descended—it does not say that there is a particular intelligible for each of us. Note that the plurality of souls and intellects asserted e.g., in Chapter 4 does not necessarily mean that there is exactly one such transcendent soul or intellect corresponding to each ordinary human being. There is considerable literature on the vexed question of Ideas of individuals in Plotinus: see Kalligas (1997) with references.

14, 22–31 *Nor are we . . . way not present.* The reference of "we" in 23 is no doubt to the empirical self, whereas "us" in the subsequent lines is to the intelligible self. The reference of "another man" is to the body with a trace (*ichnos, indalma*) of soul. See Commentary 4.6, 5–13. This man "approaches" the intelligible man and "joins" himself to him. This way of describing the matter is in harmony with the general trend in our treatise to emphasize the lower item's reaching for the higher rather than the higher descending to the lower. We find Plotinus elsewhere talking about soul descending into body (see, e.g., "On the descent of the soul into bodies" IV.8). The "approaching" and the "descent" are not meant to refer to different processes: they are different ways of describing the same phenomenon from different points of view. See Introduction, Section 2.

The outcome of this "approaching" and "joining" is a new entity, the compound of soul and body or, more precisely, compound of soul and a qualified body with a trace of soul (cf. Commentary 4.6, 5–13). This compound entity is responsible for psychic functions such as sense-perceptions that depend on the use of bodily organs. The embodied soul and the compound are discussed in detail in "The problems of soul," *passim*; see also VI.7.5, 1–5 and "What is the living being?" I.1. The fullest account of the embodied soul in Plotinus is still Blumenthal (1971).

The comparison with an ear, a voice, and an utterance (*logos*) in 26–28 resumes an analogy that has been presented more fully in Chapter 12. The ear corresponds to the body with a trace of soul, the voice bearing an utterance (*logos*) corresponds to the soul. This makes the compound analogous to an ear actually hearing.

14, 29–31 *We have become . . . way not present.* The word
"we" in 29 refers to the empirical self. These lines assert
that sometimes we are just the compound of soul and
body and not the prior intelligible Man that we were
before (cf. 18), when the latter is idle or in other ways
not present. This confirms the fluctuating nature of our
consciousness: we may at one time be preoccupied with
the body or other mundane business and entirely unaware
of our intelligible self. At times, when our thoughts
are raised to the intellect, we do not notice our bodily
nature. Plotinus takes such observations further, claiming
that what we put our mind to and eyes on determines
our identity: we become what we regard (cf. IV.4.2, 7;
IV.4.3, 6–10). This may be easier to explain as regards
intelligibles than sensibles because in the former case
Plotinus can appeal to the Aristotelian doctrine that the
subject thinking objects without matter is identical with
its objects. So if the soul thinks intelligibles, it becomes
these intelligibles. See Commentary 5.7, 1–6. This idea is
widespread in the *Enneads*. Plotinus, however, often also
suggests that by being preoccupied with the body and
the sensible realm our identity changes. Clearly, identity
here is intended in a loose sense: we become differently
disposed (cf. IV.4.3, 8) and our soul is a different sort of
soul in a crucial way.

Chapter 15

Human good and evil explained in terms of the extent to which the individual soul manages the body and the soul-body compound.

This chapter directly continues the previous one, beginning with a more detailed account of what the "approaching" in the previous chapter amounts to.

15, 1–8 *But how has . . . and its impact*: Once again, we see the application of the principle of reception according to the capacity of the recipient. Not every kind of animal receives soul equally but according to its capacity or aptitude (*epitēdeiotēs*). (See Introduction, Section 3, and Commentary 4.4, 6–12.) The comparison with an utterance in 6–8 makes explicit what may have lain in the background of the discussion of the utterance in Chapter 12 that not everyone hears what is said equally, some hear an articulate voice, others merely noise.

15, 8–18 *When the animal . . . has come to be*: These lines present more details about the nature of the composite human being. We see here some distinctions at work: (1) There is the body which is "not without a share of soul" and has acquired a trace (*ichnos*) of soul (15). On this notion see above (Commentary 4.6, 5–13). (2) There is our soul itself, which the animal (*to zōon*), i.e., the soul-body compound, "has present to it from being" (9).

15, 18–40 *The soul which . . . another, evil one*: As has been said, the whole of soul is present but it may be only partly activated (1–7). The different degree of approaching and reception is the explanation of the different ranks of souls and living beings. This does not fully explain good and evil, however, to which Plotinus now gradually turns.

Here he gives his account of the human condition: the living body has all sorts of needs to stay alive; it is unstable, vulnerable and impressionable by external blows. The body is the source of pleasures and pains, and it is liable to pull the individual soul "down," i.e., to seek to make its concerns the concerns of the whole soul. The soul itself, in its turn, is by its own nature quite undisturbed by the turmoil made by the animated body. It may, however, be carried away by this or it may take the lead and persuade the lower entity to heed reason (cf. VI.8.1–6). It is here that the analogy of the assembly and the excited mob comes in. It hardly needs any explanation but it enables us to guess Plotinus' social and political sympathies. There is a similar analogy in IV.4.17, 19–35.

By the end of the chapter (32–33) it has become clear in what "the vice of the human being" consists: like for the Plato of the *Republic,* though without the details of Plato's tripartite model of human motivation, the lower, the bodily element takes over the rule of the whole. The ultimate reason for this is that the body has matter and is close to matter; matter, in turn, is the root of evil because of its insatiety and lack of form and order (I.8.3). Even in this case, Plotinus clearly wishes to keep the individual soul unaffected. The problem is not that the individual soul is corrupt but rather that it is not heard (31). For more on this topic of the emotions and the soul's freedom from affection, see III.6.1–6 and VI.8.1–6.

Chapter 16

Periodic embodiments and descent of soul into body. The communion with the body constitutes evil for the soul because it becomes a partial soul and its activity is no longer directed toward the whole. The soul can be freed through philosophy.

Here Plotinus addresses the question raised at the beginning of Chapter 14 about the ethical differences between souls from an eschatological point of view. It turns out that in a way the original question is badly put: the souls themselves are not bad, the evil is rooted in the body (according to I.8 ultimately in matter), and moreover the organisms differ in their fitness to receive soul. The latter gives an answer to the question of different ranks among ensouled beings. All the eschatological themes there—descent of the souls, ascent, periodicity of incarnations, animal transmigration, and liberation through philosophy are mentioned in 2–4 and eventually addressed.

16, 1–7 *But if that . . . what they say*: There still remain the eschatological questions, which are a part of Plotinus' Platonic heritage: why are there "the periodic descent and subsequent ascent of the soul, and the judgments to which it is subject, and its entries into the bodies of other animals" (cf. *Phaedrus* 246a–252c and *Phaedo* 81c–d)? Plotinus feels obliged to consider how his account of embodiment fits with Platonic doctrines about periodic descents and ascents of soul and transmigration of souls into animal bodies. As we may surmise from his introductory words to this theme, these eschatological aspects of Plato's teaching do not constitute a central or prominent part of his own doctrines. Respect for Plato, however, requires that he consider these matters. The ancient philosophers referred to in 4 are no doubt Plato—Plotinus elsewhere speaks of "the ancients" in the plural when he is discussing particular Platonic passages (cf. Tornau *ad loc.*)—but perhaps also others, in particular the Pythagoreans (cf. V.1.9, 28–32.)

16, 10–13 *Clearly one must . . . that communion is*: For "coming" in 11 cf. *Phaedrus* 248e. Plotinus interprets this not as a change of place in a literal sense but as the participation of the qualified body in soul and life. (See also Commentary 4.12, 33–50.) The word "communion" (*koinonia*) is here used to refer to the communion of soul and body, which is the result of this participation.

16, 17–21 *And there is . . . sort of nature*: By "fixed order" (*taxis*) Plotinus must mean the order in which different sorts of bodies at different places receive souls.

16, 22–36 *But this sort . . . were, in potency*: The embodied soul becomes a partial soul (23), meaning that it becomes a soul in which only a part of the whole of being is active. One may wonder if this is compatible with the repeated message of earlier chapters where it is asserted that what participates in (or is present to) being or soul participates in (is present to) it as a whole. Plotinus fends off such a criticism in several ways in these lines. First, as has been repeatedly said in the treatise, the embodied soul does not belong to the part of extension that is its body. Second, activating only a part of its power does not imply that the whole power is not there. The comparison in 32–36 with actively knowing only one theorem of a science rather than the whole science supports this: someone who is actively knowing one theorem knows the whole potentially (cf. IV.9.5, 7–28 and 4.2 Commentary).

16, 28–32 *So too the . . . for the whole*: We suggest with Tornau that the two first occurrences of the word "part" here refer to the part that the soul is, i.e., that of the whole which it activates, whereas the third occurrence refers to the body, a part of the sensible cosmos.

16, 32–35 *For each particular . . . way the whole*: Here
it may seem to be asserted that souls are ultimately
individuated by embodiment, i.e., by their different
bodies. In Chapter 4, 1ff., however, there are said to be
individual, or at least different, souls and even intellects
in the intelligible realm. How are these claims to be
reconciled? The best we can come up with is that there
are two different criteria of individuation at work here.
Clearly, Plotinus holds that there are different souls
(and different beings and intellects) in the intelligible
realm (the criteria of individuation for these are nowhere
spelled out). It is compatible with this individual identity
of soul that a given such soul now enters Pythagoras'
body, at another time Socrates'. (Cf. V.7.1, 6–10; there is
also a relevant discussion in IV.3.5 but really inconclusive
as far as the exact relation between individual embodied
souls and their intelligible counterparts is concerned.)
If we then raise the question: is it Pythagoras' soul or
Socrates', in one way the answer is that it is the soul of
both. This implies that Socrates' transcendent soul is not
exclusively his soul. If we, however, consider the question
from a synchronic perspective, the answer may well be
that the body individuates the soul: it is because this soul
is set over that body and is activated accordingly that it
counts as a different soul from that other one set over the
neighboring body.

16, 37–41 *Its coming to . . . the shade is.* These lines and their sequel show Plotinus' rather relaxed attitude toward mythological material such as stories about Hades: his main concern is that his teaching is not incompatible with them. He gives two possible interpretations of the ancient claims that the souls go to Hades after death: either this means simply the separation of the soul from the body at death or it means that they go to some worse place. The first alternative is based on the ancient etymological explanation of the name "Haidēs" as "aidēs," "unseen," "invisible" (cf. Plato, *Phaedo* 81c and *Cratylus* 403a). In this case the soul is simply liberated from the body and exists by itself.

What Plotinus says about the other alternative, that the soul goes to some worse place, is far from lucid. The first response is that there would be nothing surprising in that since even now it is said to be wherever the body is—note that he says "said to be": he has been telling us repeatedly that the soul isn't really in the body. It is not clear what he means by this. Presumably, he is suggesting that being in body already is being in a bad place. He then raises the question what happens if the body no longer exists and responds with another question: "If the shade [*eidōlon*] has not been withdrawn from it [the soul], why would it not be where the shade is?" (40–41). He does not tell us where the shade might be.

In the background here seems to be the story of Odysseus
visiting the underworld and seeing the shade (*eidōlon*)
of Heracles, even if Heracles himself had found a place
among the immortals (Homer, *Odyssey* 11, 601–603).
Heracles himself among the gods symbolizes for Plotinus
the freed soul. On Plotinus' use of this myth see Pépin
(1971). We are, however, no closer to knowing the
nature of the shade. Tornau *ad loc.* interprets the "shade"
(*eidōlon*) spoken of here as the trace of soul (*ichnos
psychēs*) mentioned in 4.15, 15 (see Commentary 4.6,
5–13). If the shade is the trace of soul, it depends on the
body and is mortal. So the only way for it to continue to
exist when the body no longer exists would be through
a new incarnation. Tornau takes this to be alluded to in
39–41. We are not convinced that the shade here is to
be identified with the trace of soul, however. At least in
IV.4.27–31, where the shade and the Heracles story also
are invoked, the shade is clearly the lower soul, an entity
genuinely of the order of soul as is shown by the fact that
it has its proper memories. The same holds for I.1.12,
24ff., yet another place that alludes to the Homeric
shade of Heracles. There is no compelling reason for
understanding the shade differently here. This lower
soul, however, is essentially embodied, so that Tornau's
point about a new embodiment may still hold. Yet another
possibility, hinted at by Smith (1974, 72; cf. Appendix 2),
is that as in Porphyry's *Sententiae* 29, the shade is the

heavenly, pneumatic body the souls first acquire on their descents through the spheres (cf. IV.3.15), and the soul accompanies this body to some sort of underworld. If so, that would be the only place in the *Enneads* where the existence of Hades as a real place is asserted. We must settle on the verdict that Plotinus' meaning here is far from clear.

41–42 *But if philosophy . . . dependent on it*: There is the possibility, however, that the individual soul be freed from its shade through philosophy. That the soul can be liberated through philosophy is a view Plato expresses a number of times and Plotinus firmly believes in (cf. *Phaedo* 82e; 84a; see also *Phaedrus* 249c; *Republic* 10.619d; Plotinus: III.6.5, 1; III.7.6, 32; and IV.4.30, 24).

16, 45–48 *So much for . . . our original discussion*: The reference to the soul "illuminating itself" presumably means that the soul is concerned with itself and the intelligible rather than with illuminating the body. The claim in 47 that when freed from the body "the soul is no longer actual" may seem strange. The meaning is no doubt that it no longer acts with respect to those particular powers that were active in the embodiment.

Commentary on
Ennead *VI.5*

Chapter 1

There is a common conception about the god in each of us:
numerically one and the same god is present in many. This is
the firmest principle that our souls proclaim and the same as
the universal desire for the good, which is to be found within
ourselves.

In this very important chapter, Plotinus returns to the
main theme of the treatise: the undivided presence of
the intelligible and how this can be rendered intuitively
credible. There are some new elements in the account
given here: First, there is the identification of this
undivided presence with the divine in each of us. That there
is something divine in us is asserted by the major philosophers: Plato, Aristotle and the Stoics assert this as well

commonly received opinion. Secondly, the undivided presence is here connected with well-known Plotinian themes of desire for unity and, which turns out to be the same thing, desire for self.

1, 1–8 *A common conception . . . from this unity*: Plotinus claims that it is a common conception (*koinē ennoia*) that the god in each of us is one and the same. The expression "common conception" refers to a technical notion originating in Stoic thought and already well before Plotinus adopted by some Platonists. A common conception is a conception that every human being is supposed to develop and assent to naturally, without the aid of active learning or thinking. Sallustius, a 4th century CE Platonist philosopher, defines common conceptions as: "those conceptions to which all men will assent if questioned properly" (*De diis et mundo* 1.2, 1–2), which closely mirrors Plotinus' understanding of a common notion here. How can Plotinus claim that a belief in one and the same god in each of us is a common notion in this sense? As Tornau suggests, the answer is presumably that he is referring to a phrase of Euripides', fr. 1018, that became a well-known commonplace to which everyone would unthinkingly assent: "Our intellect is a god in each of us." He takes it that in this form at least everyone will intuitively assent to the claim about the presence of something numerically the same in many. Despite insinuating that the faith in this common conception may not survive logical scrutiny (6–7), he goes on to give a metaphysical grounding of it.

1, 8–21 *Indeed, this is . . . belongs to us*: These lines provide a continuous argument for the primacy of this principle: it is the firmest of all principles (8–9). The grounding brings in Plotinian tenets familiar from other treatises. Simply put, the reasoning is as follows: every nature is essentially a unity; some natures, however, fall short of what they essentially are; every nature, however, strives to be itself, that is, strives to be what it essentially is, that is, unity; hence, every soul strives for the unity which is itself and which it finds within itself. A very similar pattern of reasoning is also to be seen in the relationship between Intellect and the One, cf. e.g., V.3.11.

Plotinus claims that the common notion of one and the same god in each of us is the "firmest of all principles" (9). This phrase is used by Aristotle about the principle of non-contradiction (*Metaphysics* 4.1005b11–12; 1006a4–5). By using this phrase Plotinus is without doubt insinuating that his "common conception" is even more fundamental. He does not enter into a comparison of this with the principle of non-contradiction. He does say, however, that his principle is more firm than the principle that "all things desire the Good" (10–11)—presumably, another reference to Aristotle, cf. *Nicomachean Ethics* I.1 1094a1–3. In 11 he tries to justify this claim. He claims that the latter principle really presupposes the common conception. What we get in terms of justification of this, however, seems rather to be an argument for the equivalence of these two principles. For in fact, Plotinus refers to his first principle both as "the Good" and "the One." One would think, therefore, that the desire for unity and the desire for goodness must in the end be one and the same desire (cf. Tornau *ad loc.*).

1, 14–20 *For that unity . . . to be one*: These lines can be seen as an argument for the primacy of the notion of unity in relation to that of goodness, or perhaps better: the notion of good can be analyzed in terms of that of unity. Here it is said that the good consists in becoming oneself, which is the same thing as becoming one. The underlying idea, the same idea as that which underlies much of Plotinus' metaphysics of the One, Intellect, and Soul, is that because of a loss of unity, everything except the One itself is somehow deficient and not quite itself. Hence, the good for each such thing consists in regaining unity—and itself—in so far as it can. Hence, it may be said that unity is the fundamental notion that explains what is good for the different kinds of being.

The "ancient nature" spoken of in 16 is no doubt the soul. The allusion here is to *Timaeus* 90c–d, where "the divine in us," that is, the rotation of the same, which Plotinus identifies with Intellect, is called the soul's "ancient nature." (Cf. also *Republic* 10.611c–d, which talks about the "ancient nature" of Glaucus, as it was before becoming encrusted, and likens it to the disembodied soul.)

Plotinus says "every nature is striving for this unity" (17–18). A question arises about the extension of this claim: does this include sticks and stones as well as souls and intellects? While it would make sense to maintain that on the Plotinian view of things everything, even matter and bodies, strives after its own intelligible cause, this is true of souls, and in particular of the individual human soul, in a special way. As is clear from, e.g., 4.1, forms in matter have lost their ties to their intelligible causes and have become "something of the body." The general context here is also that of the individual human being, "the god in each of *us*." Even if Plotinus formulates himself very generally here and speaks of "every nature," the reference is presumably not meant to apply to beings below the level of soul.

1, 20–26 *It is in . . . things are one*: The argument here is fairly straightforward: we seek the good within ourselves because the good for us is in being and so are we, that is,

our soul belongs to that realm. So the soul will find its
good within itself.

That the Good "belongs to us" (*oikeion*) (20–21) is an
idea traceable to Socrates and Plato (cf. *Lysis* 222c3–4
and *Symposium* 205e6–7). It was adopted by the Stoics
(SVF 3.86 = Stobaeus II.69.11).

Chapter 2

The power of reasoning can derive its principles either from the objects of sense or from intelligibles. When dealing with intelligibles we must in our reasoning use principles that are proper to them.

This chapter deals with methodology. It develops the view evoked in 5.1, 5–6 that the thesis about one and the same in many cannot be properly grasped by reasoning (*logos*). The explanation is that on the one hand the power of reasoning is in a way double: a part of it derives its principles from the nature of bodies, another part of it from the nature of intelligibles. Our failure in the case at hand is that we apply reasoning proper to bodies to intelligibles. The explanation of this, in turn, is presumably that we are dealing with intelligibles present to bodies and, hence, cannot resist applying principles proper to bodies to them.

2, 1–9 *But reasoning, in . . . to true substance*: Plotinus declares that our difficulties (no doubt our difficulties with seeing how one and the same can be present to many without being divided) have to do with the power of reasoning (*logos*). This power, he says, is divided in two. We only get a glimpse of what the one of the parts of the division is toward the end of the chapter (22ff.). The other part takes its principles from the nature of bodies. This means that it takes for granted a spatio-temporal division followed by lack of identity between the different parts. The fault with his kind of reasoning when it is applied to intelligibles is that it divides substance into parts and we disbelieve in its unity. This gives false results, since souls are substances and cannot be so divided. Inquiry into intelligibles must, if one is to arrive at conviction about it, proceed from intelligible principles that are proper to it (6–9). The general idea that inquiry must start from "proper principles" (*archai oikeiai*) is Aristotelian (cf. *Posterior Analytics* 72a5–7 and Tornau *ad loc.*). By "substance" (*ousia*) here Plotinus presumably means nothing other than being.

2, 9–18 *For since there . . . from probable premises*: We see first in these lines the traditional Platonic divide between a realm of substance (*ousia*) and being, on the one hand, and a realm of becoming on the other. As regards reasoning about the latter realm, which is "in motion and admits all sorts of changes and is always spread out over all places" (10–11), it is reasonable to start from probable premises and employ probable syllogisms (17–19). In the background of these statements is the *Timaeus* 29b1–d3 account of the sphere of becoming and the epistemological constraints caused by the unstable nature of this sphere, which restrict our cognitive abilities to what is likely. This Platonic background is combined with Aristotelian epistemological and logical views. Plotinus takes the Aristotelian view that true scientific knowledge is of that which cannot be otherwise and identifies that sphere with the intelligible realm; the sensible sphere is changeable and subject to merely probable reasoning.

2, 19–28 *But when one . . . everything to it*: There are two points made in these lines. First, a repetition of the point made in 5–6 about the necessity of choosing premises from the proper domain and not making the fallacy of taking them from an alien domain. Secondly (22ff.), the soul/being turns upon itself, that is, principles proper to itself. Since it holds universally that an inquiry starts from the what-it-is, that is, the substance (cf. Aristotle, *Metaphysics* 13.4.1078b24–25), and knowing the substance brings knowledge of most of the accidents (cf. Aristotle, *On the Soul* [*De Anima*], 1.1.402b25–403a2), one should hold on to this principle of inquiry even more strongly in the case of intelligibles where there are no accidents and everything is included in the substance. For we are bound to learn everything included in the substance and there are no accidents; so the thing will be completely known.

The distinction in this chapter between two kinds of reasoning, one suitable to sensibles, the other to intelligibles, is related to a distinction that is quite pervasive in Plotinus between discursive and non-discursive (or intuitive) thought (*noēsis*). Intelligibles are properly grasped only through intuition, while reasoning (*dianoia, logos*) is the mode of thought fit for the dispersed, volatile nature of the sensible realm. For this distinction, see Emilsson (2007, ch. 4), with references. We do not, however, see evidence of the full-blown theory of intuition here, which among other things demands an intuitive, all-at-once grasp of the subject matter. In previous chapters, Plotinus has repeatedly blamed our tendency to think of soul as if it were a body for our inability to understand how one and the same can be present to many. Bodies are "always spread out over all places," which implies that each bodily part is numerically distinct from any other. Souls and intelligibles generally do not share this feature and should not be conceived in the light of principles based on it.

Chapter 3

The nature of the intelligible presented through principles proper to it. Alternative views on it rejected.

3, 1–5 *If, then, this . . . proceed from it*: Even if these lines repeat points that have been well hammered in previously, especially in 4.2–4, Plotinus evidently thinks that the intervening discussion, and in particular the points made in the previous chapter, enable us to see these tenets in a new light. Thus, the long antecedent in the conditional sentence he begins with lists many of the central claims made in previous chapters about soul and being, and the consequent concludes that "necessarily, if it is like this, it is always together with itself and does not distance itself from itself, and it is not the case that part of it is here and part there, nor does anything proceed from it" (3–5). He sees this as an inference from "proper principles" about the nature of being insisted on in the previous chapter. The words "it has been said" in 3 refer back to 4.3, 12–16.

3, 5–12 *For if it . . . not by itself*: In these lines we meet again the notion of "being in" in the sense of "depending on" familiar from 4.2. Plotinus notes in 5ff. that if being were in something else, it would be spatially dispersed and affectable. Thus, if something is "in" body in the sense of "depending on body," for Plotinus the more ordinary sense of "being in," that is, "being locally present in," follows: qualities (forms in matter) depend on their bodies in the sense of becoming something of the bodies and are located there where the body is and divided along with it. See Commentary 4.1, 15–24.

The argument presented here is a *reductio ad absurdum*. Plotinus arrives at the contradiction that being both exists by itself and does not exist by itself (12) from the supposition that something proceeds from being which, hence, would be in something else (6). As is apparent from 6, this is the premise to be rejected. The argument itself is unnecessarily complicated: it seems that Plotinus could have reached the same conclusion by merely pointing out that if being proceeded from itself and came to be in the many, it would be affected, that is, changed, which contradicts the premise about the nature of being stated in 1.

In these lines Plotinus clearly rejects the statement that something proceeds (*proienai*) from being. "Procession" is, however, one of the central terms of his double act theory: the external act is often said to proceed from the internal one. For this theory, see Introduction, Section 5. There is no need to suppose, however, that Plotinus is rejecting the double act theory here. He is wary of such language here, since it can be taken to suggest division of the intelligible. It is important to remember, however, that according to the double act theory at least as it applies to intelligibles, the external act is *not cut off from* its source, whereas here Plotinus is clearly taking procession to imply that what proceeds is cut off from its source. On the significance of this see Introduction, Section 5.

3, 13–15 *The only remaining . . . present to it*: We see in 13–15 the familiar doctrine of reception according to capacity: the many (bodies), those that are able to and to the extent they are able, participate in being (soul). On this doctrine, see Commentary 4.3, 6–12 and Introduction, Section 3.

3, 15–18 *Accordingly, it is . . . nature and substance*: The hypotheses, principles, nature, and substance spoken of here are, of course, those concerning being.

3, 20–32 *Is absent from . . . the other nature*: Having stated his positive doctrine that the source is present as a whole to the participants, Plotinus, in the midst of a sentence in 20, turns to alternatives that he does not accept.

The phrase in 21, "has no need of flowing forth," is another denial of the kind of emanation which holds that that which "flows forth" is cut off from its source (see Commentary 5.3, 5–12). The structure of the sentence and argument is: "a thing one and the same in number" has no need of going forth, neither by giving off parts "nor by itself remaining . . ." Plotinus does not justify the rejection of giving off parts, but it has been rejected in 4.4 and 4.9.

The phrase "nor by itself remaining whole while something else has left it to come out to the many scattered things" in 22–23 marks the beginning of a new (unacceptable) hypothesis. This hypothesis will occupy Plotinus throughout the chapter, except for the last sentence. As Tornau remarks *ad loc.*, the same hypothesis has been discussed previously in 4.4, 7–11 and 4.9, 7–25. See Commentary on these passages. The hypothesis is that the source, being, does not leave itself at all, that is, it remains by itself, but it gives off something else that is not being and is scattered over the many. Thus, it means to preserve the integrity of the intelligible while avoiding the presence of being to the many.

The first objection to this hypothesis in 24–26 is that the source would "have a place at a distance from those things that have come from it." It is hard to see a serious objection here. Tornau (*ad loc.*) believes that the objection is simply that by invoking "leaving" the source and the offshoot "coming out to the many," the hypothesis has attributed a location to the source. But why could not the source be without location, even if an offshoot from it is located? After all, Plotinus holds that *bodies*, which are located, have a non-located intelligible cause.

Secondly, in 26ff. Plotinus asks whether such a given offshoot is a whole or a part, that is, whether it contains everything of the original source or only a part of it. The latter alternative is discarded with reference to what has been said previously (27). As Tornau notes *ad* 5.4, 27, this probably refers back to 4.3, 31–35 and 4.8, 43 and not to 4.9, 16–18 referred to by HS$_2$. On the other hand, if each offshoot, e.g., a soul, preserves the nature of the whole, the same question will arise with respect to the soul in each part of the body it animates. Does each part preserve the nature of the whole soul? If the soul is divided into spatially distinct parts along with the body (28–29), the hypothesis leads to an infinite regress, which is here merely alluded to. See above, Commentary 4.4, 11–18. If each of the offshoots is whole throughout, the hypothesis concedes Plotinus' view that the same soul is present as a whole in many bodily parts. If this is so in the case of a single soul, there is no good reason for denying that this is possible for the intelligible generally.

3, 30–32 *Note that this . . . the other nature*: This final sentence of the chapter merely summarizes the methodology employed in the chapter, undoubtedly both as regards its positive and negative conclusions, connecting them to the methodological principles expounded in 5.2. Thus, as Tornau notes *ad* 5.3, 20, these two chapters comprise a whole in terms of argumentation (cf. Commentary 5.5, 1–5).

Chapter 4

Given that god is everywhere, god cannot be portioned out like a body with a distinct part of it here, another one there. Arguments aiming to establish that being is present to everything.

This chapter does not directly continue Chapter 3 although it is connected to the previous discussion of the one god. It can be divided into two rather different sections both in terms of content and rhetoric. The former section, 1–13, resumes the popular appeal to everybody's notion of the divine from 5.1. In the second half, 13–24, Plotinus enters into a complicated but elliptical metaphysical argument aiming to establish that the One (god) is present to everything.

4, 1–5 *Observe also the . . . we hold this*: What is said in these lines, which pick up the theme of divine omnipresence from 5.1, is meant to dispel distrust in Plotinus' central claim about undivided omnipresence: given that god is everywhere (as presumably anyone is supposed to admit), god cannot be portioned out like a body with a distinct part of itself here, another one there.

The appeal to the notion of all who have a notion of god in support of the statement that there is nowhere where he is not, may be rooted in Stoicism, as Tornau *ad loc.* suggests. And as noted above (Commentary 5.1, 1–8), the very idea of "common conceptions" is Stoic and there are also Stoic sources claiming that god is everywhere (cf. LS 47 O = SVF 2.634 and LS 47 = SVF 2.441). Plotinus could also cite traditional texts that at least vaguely support his view, e.g., Hesiod, *Works and Days*, 253ff. and 267ff., which describe Zeus's power to see, hear and think everything. How could he, if he was not everywhere?

4, 5–13 *But if god . . . as a whole*: Plotinus here argues from the weaker claim, which presumably everyone will admit, that god or the gods are everywhere, to the stronger claim that god is everywhere as a whole. The crucial part of the argument for this is that if this were not the case, god would not be one but divided. Furthermore, if this were the case, god would be a body, which is absurd. These two claims may be connected. One might think that if god is everywhere but with different parts in different regions, he is nevertheless one because he is continuous. Plotinus remarks about bodies that they have unity only in the sense of continuity (IV.2.1, 59–60). That sort of unity, however, clearly does not suffice for him here: he appeals to the intuition that if only, say, 1/8 of god is here but no whole god, god has been divided and is not really everywhere: to be everywhere in the intuitive sense implies that the whole of god is everywhere.

4, 13–17 *Again, if we . . . it is not*: A new argument begins here. It is rather sketchy. A fuller version has already been given in 4.5, 1–11. It takes as a premise that "that nature" is unlimited (*apeiron*) in the sense of inexhaustible and seeks to derive the conclusion that it is present to everything. Presumably, the reference of "that nature" is to the nature of the intelligible generally, which he here takes to be the same as god and gods. He frequently calls both the One and Intellect gods. (See, e.g., I.1.8, 9; V.1.6, 9; VI.9.5, 3 [the One]; I.8.7, 15; IV.3.11, 11; V.8.3, 23–24 [Intellect].)

4, 17–24 *For indeed, should . . . present as well*: The interpretation of these lines poses a challenge. Most translators, including Bréhier, HBT, and Armstrong, take the occurrence of "the one itself" (*auto to hen*) in 17 to refer to the One, the first principle. However, "the one" does not always refer to the One. (Parallel difficult questions about the reference of "the one" or "the good" arise in a number of places in the *Enneads*.) There is also a question of what is understood to go with the verb "say." With HBT, Cilento, and Tornau, the translation here supposes the verb "*pareinai*," "to be present," to be understood from 15. Tornau (*ad loc.*), allowing that both alternatives are possible, however, argues that "the one" in 17 is still the intelligible being which has been the topic. The main reason he gives for this preference is that it fits the context better. The tentativeness of the beginning of the sentence, "For indeed, should we say" (*kai gar ei legoimen*), suits badly the supposition that it is a question of the first principle. For Plotinus it is a matter of course that something else comes after the One. Nevertheless, it seems that the words "the one itself" would be a strange and unexpected way to refer to the intelligible being, and we opt for translating *to hen* as "the One." The tentative character of "should we say" is unproblematic if "to be present" is understood, for what is tentatively suggested here is not that something comes after the One but that something other than the One is present to the many, something that comes after it. Perhaps the distinction between god and the gods earlier in the chapter (3–4) foreshadows this distinction between the One here and what comes after the One. In any case, if what has been suggested here is right, the point Plotinus is making is that even if what comes to be present to the many is not the One itself but something that comes after it, that is, Intellect or Soul, what comes after the One is so close to it that what participates in the former also participates in the latter.

4, 20–24 *For since there . . . present as well*: In these final lines of the chapter, Plotinus begins to describe the different ranks in the intelligible world with the aid of an illustration of a circle and its center, which he continues in the next chapter. He often refers to soul, Intellect, and the One collectively as the intelligible, *to noēton*, even if the One is not, strictly speaking, intelligible. The reference to the things of third, second, and first rank is without doubt to soul, Intellect, and the One. The reference to the One is given in the plural (*ta prōta*), which may be surprising given that the One is a singularity. The explanation is probably that he is picking up a phrase from Plato's 2nd Letter 312e1–4.

Chapter 5

The center of a circle and radii going from it is introduced as an analogy of the relationship between the One, intelligibles, and sensibles.

An analogy of the circle, its radii, and center, occupies this entire chapter. As indicated by the word "often" in 1, this is an analogy Plotinus commonly uses. He does not only employ it to illustrate the relation between the One and the intelligibles as here (cf. also III.8.8, 36–38; V.1.11, 10–13; IV.3.17, 12–16; VI.8.18, 1–22), but also other relationships between an overarching intelligible nature and subordinates: the indivisible and the divisible (in relation to *Timaeus* 35a: IV.1, 15–17); the soul and the sensory powers (IV.7.6, 11–15); eternity and time (III.7.3, 19; VI.5.11, 18–21).

The origins of Plotinus' use of these circle analogies have been traced to Peripatetic psychology. Henry (1960) suggests that Aristotle's and especially Alexander of Aphrodisias' concerns with the unity of conscious sense-perception served as sources for Plotinus here (cf. Aristotle, *De Anima* III, 427a10–13 and Alexander of Aphrodisias, *De Anima*, 61–63). In developing Aristotle's thought, Alexander actually speaks of the center and the radii of a circle: the soul is both one and many as the center of the circle: it is one in being the unique point in which all the different senses meet; it is many in being the end point of the different radii (63, 8–13). Indeed, it seems likely that Plotinus was inspired by Alexander here, whom we know from Porphyry's *Life of Plotinus* (*Vita Plotini*) 14 to have been read in Plotinus' school. As Tornau points out, however, Plotinus may have been inspired by other circle models as well, such as those in Plato, e.g., the *Timaeus* account of the circular movement of the soul. To this Stoic sources may be added, e.g., the idea of concentric circles encompassing each of us (cf. Hierocles in Stobaeus, 4.671, 7–673, 11 = LS 57 G).

Here the center clearly represents the One. The picture is otherwise fairly complex. It is not the case, for instance, that the center of a circle simply represents the One and the radii falling out from the center represent the other intelligibles. Plotinus makes a point of insisting that we have on the one hand the center of the circle, and then the superimposed end-points of the radii, all meeting at the center and coinciding with each other and the center at that point. There are two distinct messages Plotinus wishes to convey with this: (1) there is a single, incorporeal source of the intelligibles (and hence of everything else); (2) the intelligibles are indeed many but they are "all together" and not spatially distinct. It seems that the picture of the center of a circle is apt to convey (1) but unless modified, the circle image may not do justice to (2) because of the spatial distinctness of the radii in circumference from the center. It may be for this reason that Plotinus complicates the picture with the idea of superimposed starting points of the radii at the center: the superimposition does away with the spatial differentiation otherwise suggested by the circle (cf. Tornau *ad loc.*).

5, 3–10 *But in speaking . . . would be one*: What follows here and in the remainder of the commentary on this chapter is a paraphrase of the train of thought in these lines as we understand it: It is important to preserve the "all things together" character of the intelligibles (3–4; see Commentary 4.4, 23–36). The circle analogy indeed manages this in a way, since the radii form a continuous surface (6). The intelligibles, however, exhibit an even stronger togetherness than a continuous surface can represent, since they are unextended substances and powers (6–7). Hence, if we stick to the analogy, the intelligibles rather correspond to the starting points of the radii at the center, where they all meet, as it were, superimposed on one another, having left the lines, that is, the radii, behind (7–10).

5, 11–17 *If one were . . . all be one*: Suppose we extend the lines again towards the periphery of the circle. The starting points of the radii would still be in contact with and not cut off from "the one original center" (13–14), which clearly represents the One itself. The intelligibles are many, as the radii, but in a sense all one, which fact is signified in that they all unite in a point.

5, 17–23 *If, then, we . . . in many places*: The lines (radii) here, each pointing in a different direction, stand for the intelligibles' activity in different spatial regions.

Chapter 6

*In acting on the sensible a partial intelligible becomes active,
however containing the whole. This is illustrated from the
case of the Idea of man and particular human beings.*

6, 1–3 *For the intelligibles . . . "all are together"*: This
chapter directly continues the previous one, as is seen
from the connective "for." The end of the previous
chapter suggests that the radii of the circle are to their
end-points as the sensible realm is to the intelligible
nature. This is indeed what we will see in the present
chapter, but in these lines we still have the by now familiar
formulations emphasizing the unity-in-multiplicity
within the intelligible realm.

6, 3–6 *And they are . . . whole accompanies it*: With Tornau
we take 3–6 to describe the activity of the intelligible on
the sensible: the first "whole" is the sensible cosmos, the
second and the third is the whole intelligible realm. The
"partial activity" is a partial intelligible, but bringing with
it the whole intelligible realm (cf. Commentary 4.4.2).

6, 6–15 *It is as . . . being is everywhere*: The reasoning in these lines is not entirely clear and perhaps it is confused. It looks as if Plotinus wants to give us an example illustrating what he has just said or at least a comparable example (the word *hoion*, here translated as "it is as if," could also be translated simply as "for example"). However, the case of the Idea of man and the particular men—the latter apparently understood here as the enmattered human forms and not, e.g., as the human souls—does not really illustrate what he wished to illustrate, because the forms in matter don't carry the whole intelligible realm with them and indeed become something belonging to their underlying bodies (cf. 4.1, 15–24): the different signet-ring imprints are different individuals, even if they share a form. Moreover, in the last part of the chapter, 10–16, Plotinus seems to recognize this. It is as if he takes an example for comparison or illustration, and then goes on to criticize it.

In addition, there is a problem with the claim in 7–9 that the man in matter makes many identical men from the Idea of man. We are at a loss as to what is being referred to here, the notion of man in matter as a maker of other men is surely not a standard Plotinian notion. It seems he could have in mind ordinary procreation. In that case, however, the role of the Idea of man is left quite unclear.

Chapter 7

This chapter is a natural sequel but not a direct continuation of the previous one: Plotinus here returns to the relation between being and the self.

7, 1–6 *Indeed, both we . . . being in them*: We are our individual soul, which primarily operates as discursive reason busying itself with impressions from the senses (cf. Commentary 4.14, 16–29). This self, however, is also "referred (*anagetai*) back to being." This means that even our everyday empirical self has its roots in being, that is, the purely intelligible realm. Then it is further asserted that we can ascend to this realm. If we do so ascend, we become the intelligibles. In this we can detect an adoption of the Aristotelian view that in pure thought of intelligibles, that is, things without matter, the subject of the thought is identical with the objects of the thought (cf. Aristotle, *On the Soul* [*De Anima*] 430a2–3, 19; 431a1–2; *Metaphysics* 12.9.1075a3–4). The necessity of receiving an image or impression is associated with external cognition of which sense perception is the paradigmatic case (cf. V.5.1).

The intelligibles are not external to Intellect. Thus, in thinking them, the subject of the thought is thinking itself. There is, however, more to Plotinus' version of this than a mere adoption of the Aristotelian principle: the self is one of the intelligibles, not just a tourist inspecting this realm from an external point of view. There are texts emphasizing that in grasping the other intelligibles a given one also grasps itself: it sees itself, as it were, as an integral part of the realm to which it truly belongs (see, e.g., IV.4.2 and V.8.7; see further Emilsson [2007, ch. 2]).

It is somewhat unclear what Plotinus has in mind by "the first thing that comes from it [being]." Normally, the first thing that comes from being would surely be soul; now it is the soul which is said to ascend to this first thing that comes from being; but the soul is already soul, so why should it have to ascend? Presumably, the answer is that there is an undescended level of our souls (cf. Commentary 4.14, 18–22). It must be to this that our souls ascend when they ascend to this first thing that comes from being (cf. Tornau *ad loc.*).

7, 6–8 *But since others . . . are all one*: Plotinus argues that we, that is, all human beings, are in a sense one. It is clear that the reason for this is the sort of identity each of us has with the intelligible realm: each *is* it, hence each is the same thing. There are, however, at least two possibilities of understanding the details of this. It might be the case that we are all something universal, say, the Idea of man. Or it might be that each of us has something individual in the intelligible realm, but, because of the unity and holism that holds for that realm, we are nevertheless one with each other and that whole realm. This question remains unresolved. (See also Commentary 4.16, 32–35.)

7, 9–17 *Yet since we . . . everything is placed*: Here the question is raised why we as empirical selves (see Commentary 4.14, 16) are not aware of the intelligible and our identity with it. The answer is that we "look outward" and not "inward." In this capacity, we are like faces of a many-faced head, each face looking outward and away towards the sensible realm. Only if we manage to turn around and look inside, shall we see god himself and everything, that is, all the intelligibles and, moreover, see ourselves as identical with this whole intelligible realm. This view of Plotinus was rejected by later Neoplatonists, while Leibniz, who explicitly attributes it to Plotinus, praises it (G. W. Leibniz [1840]). For other expressions of this view, see, e.g., III.4.3, 22; IV.4.2 and IV.7.10, 34–36.

Lines 11–12 describe the soul's turning around towards the inside and the higher realities. Such a turn away from the body and the sensible towards the intelligible is frequently mentioned in the *Enneads*. It is what in

Plotinus corresponds to salvation and brings with it happiness (cf. I.4) and freedom (cf. VI.8). Such ideas are not new with Plotinus and can be traced back to Plato (cf. the Allegory of the Cave in *Republic* 7). Here he suggests that this may happen through one's own efforts, presumably a virtuous life and philosophical studies, or by luck if one is somehow touched and awakened by the divine realm. The reference to the goddess Athena in 12 evokes *Iliad* 1, 197, where Athena gets the attention of Achilles in battle by yanking on his hair. What is peculiar for Plotinus' version of this turning is the emphasis he puts on not merely "looking upward" but on "looking inward"; cf. also, e.g., V.1.1, 26ff.: the way to knowledge of the higher is through knowing oneself. Even if the details are quite different, we see the general trend in Descartes' *Meditations*.

What is meant by "god" in 12–13 is Intellect rather than the One: the whole passage describes a non-discursive, intellectual experience rather than the exceptional experience of a mystical union with the One. The latter is not a proper object of intellectual vision on a par with the intelligibles. Plotinus suggests that we would at first see ourselves as distinct from the whole of being but eventually merge with it, since one in this state "will not have anywhere to put himself in order to measure the extent of himself." By this last statement he presumably means that we may at first identify with the intelligibles closest to ourselves, but since the whole of the intelligible is a seamless web where each intelligible implicates every other, we won't settle down till we have fathomed the whole.

Chapter 8

The participation of matter in Ideas.

This chapter introduces a new topic, the participation of bare matter in Ideas, the result of which is the genesis of the four elements. Parts of the chapter are notoriously difficult, and editors and translators are agreed that the text is corrupt at crucial places. The difficulties lie in 22–35 and in particular in 29–33, where the delivered text clearly needs revision. HS₂ stamps these lines as unclarified in their apparatus—"locus nondum sanatus." We follow here the emendations suggested by Tornau, which in turn are partly based on proposals by others, Igal, in particular. The fact remains that the text of 29–33 is uncertain and what is suggested here is highly hypothetical.

8, 1–3 *I think that . . . difficulties about it*: The first line of this chapter "if one also were to examine the participation of matter in Forms" clearly shows that this is a new topic in relation to the foregoing and, in fact, a topic that has hardly been addressed so far in the treatise. The brief discussion of man in matter in 5.6 is not quite the same topic as this one, since here Plotinus is dealing with the original information of matter by Ideas, a topic for which *Timaeus* 48e4ff. is the most important background. In any case, Plotinus claims that his main thesis, the indivisibility of the intelligible, can be seen from consideration of this topic as well.

As Tornau notes (*ad loc.*), the way the issue of participation of matter in Forms is introduced here suggests that this is a school topic Platonists were wont to address. In fact, by Plotinus' time, Aristotelian prime matter, that is, the matter underlying the elements, had been combined with the Receptacle from Plato's *Timaeus* with the result that we have three items: the transcendent Idea, the matter, which participates in the Idea, and the result of this participation, the form in matter. The latter corresponds to Aristotelian sensible forms (cf. Alcinous, *Didaskalikos*, 162, 29ff.). Plotinus himself normally adheres to this general picture. His agendum here is to argue that the Idea itself is not divided as a result of the participation.

8, 4–15 *For I think it . . . in this way*: As a first step in arguing his case, Plotinus claims that it is a mistake to see the separation of Ideas from their participants as a spatial separation. The Idea is indeed separate from its sensible images, the forms in matter, but this separation just means that the Idea is a paradigm and is not dispersed among its participants. This passage implies that Plotinus rejects the formulation of the theory of Forms that Parmenides attributes to Socrates at *Parmenides* 130a8–b6. Hence, talk of illumination, which Plotinus admittedly has indulged in himself (11–12), is to be seen merely as suggesting separation of Ideas from sensibles, not the sort of spatial separation we have when one sensible thing illuminates another. So "separation" for Plotinus amounts to something like "different mode of being."

The words "from somewhere far above" (*anōthen pothen*) in 5 are an allusion to Plato's *Sophist* 246b7, whereas "difficult to explain" (*dysphraston*) and "most puzzling" (*aporōtaton*) in 8 allude to *Timaeus* 50c6 and 51b1.

8, 15–22 *But now we . . . remaining in itself*: We see here, yet again, the doctrine of reception according to the capacity of the recipient, pure matter being the recipient in this case. The sentence in 18–20, ". . . as if it were simultaneously both in contact and not in contact with the Idea from all directions, acquires throughout itself from the Form in virtue of its approach as much as it is able to receive . . ." poses some problems. To speak in contradictions such as we see here is a part of Plotinus' philosophical style. What he usually intends by this is that something is so and so in one way, and not in another. And what he has in mind here is presumably that the Idea is in contact with matter in the sense that it indeed imparts an image of itself on it, but it is not in contact with it in that it does not give anything of itself to matter, it remains totally unaffected by the "contact." The approach (*plēsiasmos*) of matter towards the Idea referred to here may seem puzzling because it apparently attributes some positive action to matter while according to all other sources matter is quite inert, indeed mere privation (cf. II.4.14). The answer is presumably that not only is the "approach" spoken of here to be taken without any spatial connotations, it does not even attribute any positive effort to matter: the "approach" simply indicates that matter receives as it is able to, which in fact is very little, because, even if the Ideas are "reflected" in it, it does not succeed in capturing them permanently. (See further Tornau *ad loc.* and O'Meara [1980].)

8, 22–28 *For if the . . . other so-called elements*: Here Plotinus invokes fire as an example of an element produced in matter, clearly assuming that a parallel account will hold for the other elements. The sentence in 24–26 reflects *Timaeus* 51b4–6, a passage Plotinus gives an extended interpretation of in III.6.12, 28–48.

As Tornau notes, 26–28, "Let us assume . . . other so-called elements," is significant in the context (most translators do not note this and take these remarks as somehow parenthetical): a primary character of fire, which it shares with the other elements, is that it is a "manifold mass." This is the essential characteristic of bodies as such from which follows the kind of spatial divisibility characteristic that our treatise aims at avoiding for soul and the other intelligibles.

8, 28–35 *If, then, that . . . many times over*: The vexed textual difficulties are contained within these lines. The translation and commentary here is based on the text as emended by Tornau. The part of the translated text that contains the significant emendations runs as follows: Εἰ οὖν τὸ ἓν ἐκεῖνο πῦρ ἡ ἰδέα ἐν πᾶσι θεωρεῖται παρέχον εἰκόνα ἑαυτοῦ, [καὶ] <οὐ κατὰ τὸ> τόπῳ χωρὶς ὂν [οὐ] παρέξει ὡς ἡ ἔλλαμψις ἡ ὁρωμένη· ἤδη γὰρ εἴη που πᾶν τοῦτο τὸ πῦρ τὸ ἐν αἰσθήσει, <οὐδ'> [εἰ π]ᾶν αὐτὸ πολλά <εἴη>, ἑαυτοῦ τῆς ἰδέας etc. Plotinus starts with an if-clause: "If, then, that single Fire, understood as an Idea, is seen providing an image of itself in everything." As a consequent he then proceeds to make two points, both of which specify how the if-clause is *not* to be interpreted: (1) there is no illumination, which indeed would preserve the unity of the Idea but not its transcendence, since the Idea would be given a spatial location; (2) the Idea is not itself present in the particular fires by multiplying itself: in that case, the Idea would have become many in the same way as body is many, i.e., having non-identical spatial parts.

8, 35–46 *And the Idea . . . that does so*: Here we see the by now familiar claim that the Idea gives nothing of itself to matter and, in addition, that there is no need to posit many Ideas of, say, Fire, one for each sensible fire. These two claims are no doubt connected: if "not giving something of itself to the many" implies "not giving different parts of itself to the different sensibles," the Idea as a whole will inform the many. Since this is possible and is in fact the case, there is no need to assume different Ideas for different masses of fire. In fact, since each part of a bodily mass, even of a single, continuous mass, is different from any other and there is an infinite number of such parts, an infinite number of Ideas would be needed.

Chapter 9

One and the same life animates the whole cosmos. Previous philosophers on the nature of the soul are discussed. Quantitative terms do not apply to the soul, it is one and many.

This chapter at first continues the general topic of Chapter 8, that is, the relation of matter and bodies to the intelligible realm. While in the previous chapter Plotinus expounded the nature of the relation through the example of a single Idea, he now considers the matter from a wider perspective: all the elements forming the sphere of the cosmos.

9, 1–10 *If continuing with . . . that produces it*: The point Plotinus wishes to make in these lines is that, even if the sensible cosmos contains differentiated parts, it does not follow that there is a plurality of causes. We have seen repeatedly that soul-being is undivided and the previous chapter makes it clear that the cause of the sensible phenomena lies there in the intelligible; since that is undivided, it, as a whole, is the cause, not independent partial agents. The "account" (*logos*) in 1–2 presumably refers to the account of the generation of the physical world in the *Timaeus*, starting with the elements. On Plotinus' cosmology see the treatises "On heaven" (II.1) and "On the movement of the heaven" (II.2). There is a recent English edition and translation with a commentary on the former: Wilberding (2006).

9, 10–13 *And thus one . . . unlimited in number*: "Single life" in 11 presumably just means "one soul," that is, it is in virtue of being in a single soul that the cosmos has a single life. The notion of life in Plotinus is, however, not restricted to soul. Life is also an integral feature of Intellect, and there are passages that describe the first emanation from the One as life (III.8.10, 2–3). We have then yet another statement of the claim that all souls are one. To this Plotinus adds: ". . . and [they are] one in the sense of being unlimited (*apeiros*). There are at least two senses in which the soul can be said to be unlimited: as inexhaustible, that is, never running out of life-giving power, and as without boundaries. Only this latter sense can be readily seen as an elucidation of the claim that they are all one. So there emerges a picture according to which there are indeed different souls but they form a unity because there is no absolute boundary between them (cf. Commentary 4.5, 1–11). In what follows, however, Plotinus also seems to appeal to the sense of "inexhaustible."

9, 13–31 *For this reason . . . kind of completeness*: Plotinus alludes to past philosophers' pronouncements about the soul in light of what he has said: (1) that the soul is number, Xenocrates, fr. 60 = Aristotle, *On the Soul* [*De anima*], 1.2.404b27–30) and (2) that the soul is a ratio (*logos*) increasing itself (cf. Heraclitus, B115). He seeks to interpret these claims so as to make them compatible with the main tenets of the treatise. His central point is that quantitative notions do not apply to the soul in the way they apply to bodies. Hence, the soul is not a number increasing itself in the sense that it comes to be of greater quantity along with the body. Even if the cosmos became larger, the soul would fill out the new bulk. If it is said to increase, this must mean that it is inexhaustible, that is, should the body increase, the soul will ensoul that larger body as well without losing anything (cf. VI.4.5, 18–22 and VI.5.8, 43–45).

In 24 Plotinus speaks of "the unity that attaches to truth." "Truth" in such contexts is nothing other than being or Intellect. That is to say, Plotinus understands "truth" as the genuine article as opposed to the copy and so understood it is identical with "real being." This notion of truth, however, also has associations with a mind that grasps the truth, but that mind is identical with the truth it grasps (see V.3.5, 23–26 and V.5.2, 13–24, and also Emilsson [2007], 165–170). The words in 29–30, "it does not know where on earth it is" is a tag from Plato's *Republic* 3.403e5–6.

9, 31–40 *So if its . . . everywhere in itself*: The discussion is redirected to the topic of the unity of the soul. Interestingly, Plotinus maintains that the essential unity of the soul implies an innate plurality. Plotinus formulates this in 32 in the language of Aristotelian predication theory: if X has genuine unity, "one" is predicated of it essentially, that is, being one is a feature pertaining to X's substance. The general idea behind this is no doubt that the soul is a unity-in-plurality (cf. Commentary 4.4, 18–23). It surely is not the One itself, which cannot even be said to be one, because this would imply a duality of subject and predicate (VI.9.5, 30–32). Thus, anything "one" is predicated of is by nature plural. The plurality pertaining to the soul is something that pertains to it internally and essentially, as is the case with Intellect (cf. 4.4). Sometimes Plotinus distinguishes formally the kind of unity pertaining to soul from the kind of unity pertaining to Intellect, calling the former "many and one," the latter "one-many." These epithets are supposed to correspond to the second and third hypotheses of Plato's *Parmenides* (see V.1.8, 25–26). In our treatise, however, the formal distinctions between soul and Intellect tend to be minimized. The ultimate source for the essential plurality of being in Plotinus is Plato's *Sophist* 250c7ff., where being is claimed to be one form, which always combines with others, and Plato's *Parmenides* 144b1–e7, which is reflected in 36–39.

In 37–38 he describes the soul as "a single rational formula (*logos*)," as he previously has described being: see 4.11, 15–20 and Commentary for Plotinus' notion of rational formula (*logos*). As Tornau notes, the statement that this rational formula is "a single rational formula encompassing itself" reflects Plato's *Parmenides* 145b6–c7. As the sequel indicates, the meaning seems simply to be the by now familiar idea that any "part" contains the whole.

9, 40–48 *Since it is . . . to be preserved*: We see here a reiteration of claims made several times before in the treatise: that soul is prior to anything in place and is not divided by place: things in place (bodies) need the soul to rest in but the soul does not leave itself when the bodies have taken rest in it. The talk of "foundation" and "setting up" in 45 reveals the metaphor behind Plotinus' language of "establishment" (*hidrusthai*), namely the setting up of, or dedicating, statues. This is evidently something close to his mind when thinking of giving something a place.

Chapter 10

This chapter directly continues Chapter 9, but the focus smoothly changes from the ontological issue of the soul-body relation to human beings' relation to the intelligible.

10, 1–11 *So it chastely . . . each of them*: Plotinus brings up ideas of love from the *Symposium* and *Phaedrus*. In Plato's *Symposium*, neither Eros nor ordinary lovers in this world receive beauty itself, but they are present to it and participate in it. Beauty remains in itself while the lovers desire it and it suffices for them all because it is not divided by their participation. Clearly, the suggestion is that the relation between soul and body and, more generally, between the sensible and the intelligible is like that. The reference to "Eros upon the doorsteps" in 3–4 is to Eros in need of the beautiful in *Symposium* 206c1–e3.

10, 11–27 *And indeed wise . . . was doing so*: This consideration of lovers striving after beauty leads Plotinus to wise thought (*to phronein*) and Heraclitus' saying that

wise thought is common (Heraclitus, B113). He makes
the following claims about wise thoughts: a wise thought
is something that exists in itself; if more than one thinks
the same wise thought, the thoughts in each are really
the same, that is, each of the thinkers shares the same
thought which exists in itself independently of these
thinkers. Thus, the thoughts are shared. But what exactly
does he mean by "wise thoughts" here? The Greek word
phronein is the word used in the Heraclitus fragment,
whereas what Plotinus has to say about wise thought here
fits very well with what he commonly expresses in terms
of intellection (*noein*). The thoughts of Intellect are there,
existing in their own right for anyone capable of sharing
in them. Presumably, he is just using "wise thought" in
the sense of intellection. Possibly he has in mind the wise
thought of souls that are acting on their own, informed
by Intellect and freed from all bodily involvement (cf.
Tornau *ad loc.*).

10, 27–42 *We should try . . . our own intelligibles*: Our
souls' contact with the Good (the One) is of the same
kind: we are all in contact with the same Good, which
does not send anything forth out of itself into another
thing. The sight of and contact with the Good mentioned
in 40–42 is not the so-called mystical union with the
Good (cf. Tornau *ad loc.*), nor is Plotinus claiming
a direct epistemic access to the Good: it is rather that

our intelligible selves, as other pure intelligibles, are informed and gain their self-sufficiency from their gaze at the Good, which, however, fails to capture the Good in its simplicity (cf., e.g., V.3.11). Even in the body of the sensible world, which is a single organism, there is action and affection without anything going forth into something else because there is nothing outside it (cf. *Timaeus* 33c3–d1). This is all the more evident in the case of the unextended intelligible realm. The latter realm is in fact much more unified than the sensible one in that it is free from the dispersion of spatial extension.

10, 42–52 *And there is . . . were bodily volumes*: The reference to a duplication of the sensible sphere is a humorous allusion to Aristotle's famous criticism of the Theory of Ideas as reduplication of the sensible world in *Metaphysics* 1.9.990b1–4. The "intelligible sphere" in 43–44 is based on Plotinus' interpretation of Parmenides, B8, 40–44 (cf. V.1.8, 20–22). As Parmenides himself, who describes his one being as a uniform sphere, Plotinus intends this metaphorically (cf. V.8.9, 1–12). That the intelligibles should be unified in the intelligible sphere is no surprise: we know how branches of knowledge are unified in the soul. For the comparison of the presence of branches of knowledge and theorems in the soul with intelligibles in 47ff., see above Commentary 4.2.

Chapter 11

The familiar thesis that the soul reaches over a great expanse without being divided repeated; it is said still to need assurance. The intelligible is outside time.

11, 1–4 *But how can . . . our mind's puzzlement*: Plotinus again raises the initial questions of the treatise of how the intelligible—the intelligible nature at stake here being soul—can "exceed all bodies and attain to such a magnitude," and how it can do so and retain its unity (see VI.4.1, 1–13 and Commentary).

11, 4–14 *Indeed it has . . . limited in quantity*: Plotinus notes that he has repeatedly addressed this question—as indeed he has—and demonstrated that it in fact attains such magnitude while remaining one, but further assurance is still needed (4–6). What he has to say about the matter in 6–14—pointing to the difference between the power of the intelligible and that of a stone—hardly adds anything significant to what has already been said about this. A stone is his standard example of a lifeless and inert body.

11, 14–34 *For this reason, . . . the same thing*: A new
point is raised: the intelligible is outside time. Plotinus
takes this to follow from what he has just said about its
being "in no way limited by quantity." Just as spatial
extension, time involves a fragmentation or separation
of things that exist unified at the intelligible level.
Temporal separation is thus to be seen as an aspect of
the increased fragmentation or dispersion the further an
item is removed from the One. Plotinus' views on time
are developed in some detail in IV.4.14 and especially in
his treatise "On eternity and time" (III.7). They are, as
one might expect, a development of Plato's account in the
Timaeus 37c6–38b5. There, Plato calls time the image
of eternity (*aiōn*) and asserts that the sensible world is
confined to time. Plotinus takes this even further in that
he clearly understands eternity here as timelessness rather
than merely infinite duration (cf. "wholly outside time"
in 15). On Plotinus' views on time, see Strange (1994)
and Smith (1996).

The analogy with the point and the moving radius in
18–31 is to be interpreted as follows (cf. also III.7.3, 19–
22): the point at the center, on which the radii depend,
corresponds to the intelligible realm: it is unextended
and unmoved, even if the moving radii "partake" of it.
The movement itself corresponds to time whereas the
distance from the center signifies the extent to which a

given entity is removed from its intelligible source. In general this circle analogy serves the same function as the circle analogy in 5.5, that is, to illustrate the intelligible-sensible relation. In the present version, however, the immobility of the center vs. the movement of the radii is meant to capture the dependence of the temporal on the atemporal.

As evidenced in 22–34, extension in time and extension in space function in this way analogically, and Plotinus uses the same vocabulary for both kinds of dispersion. There is dependence of the temporal on the atemporal, as the *Timaeus* account indeed suggests. Also the doctrine of reception according to the capacity of the recipient is applied to explain the temporal: because of its weakness the recipient cannot receive everything at once but takes as much as it is fit to take. Plotinus then goes on to explain in 34–38 that nevertheless the whole intelligible nature is present to all in the same way as the Idea of the triangle is present to every material triangle, that is, one and the same undivided for all. The implication seems to be that the temporally distinct items of the same kind, e.g., present and future material triangles, are different ontological items.

11, 31–38 *It is present . . . to every matter*: These lines follow directly the discussion of timelessness as a part of

the same discussion but they raise a new point: why isn't
the enmattered triangle everywhere? This is an extremely
pertinent question. One could wish for a more detailed
discussion of it. The pertinence of the question lies in the
fact that Plotinus has repeatedly emphasized the role of
the different capacities of the recipient in accounting for
the differences between the phenomena. Prime matter
is presumably undifferentiated on Plotinus' account, so
why should some of it receive an image of this Idea, and
another part the image of another Idea? Here he points
out that not even prime matter receives everything but
only the four elements (here called the "primary kinds"),
which then become the recipients of other forms. This
response, however, only postpones the problem because
the question arises again: why does something become fire
and something else water? Presumably, the answer is that
we should not expect the doctrine of reception according
to capacity to explain every difference. Ultimately,
something in the structure and nature of the intelligible
itself also plays a role. This topic, however, is nowhere
researched in Plotinus. See Introduction, Section 3.

Chapter 12

The intelligible whole is present to the sensible as a single life.
The experience of abandoning the other things described: the
human soul can grasp the whole intelligible realm and itself
as an integral part of it by abandoning non-being.

This last chapter does not add much in terms of philosophical content to what has already been presented. It
does, however, eloquently summarize—Plotinus even
employs some rare poetical words—the main contentions
of the treatise and relates them to the individual soul.
It shines through that he considers the individual soul's
capacity—a capacity that is not diminished by the soul's
embodiment—to identify with the whole intelligible
realm as the most important lesson of the foregoing
chapters.

12, 1–7 *How, then, is . . . it gets smaller*: In these lines
the main point is the already familiar inexhaustibility of
the intelligible: its power is unchanged by changes in
the quantity of the bulk it animates (cf. VI.4.5, 11–22

and Commentary). On the intelligible being present "as a single life" (*zōē mia*), see 5.9, 11 and Commentary. There is a textual problem in 6, a place HS₂ considers unresolved. The translation here follows Igal's (1975, 185) emendation of the delivered text to *ekei hylēn*, "there matter," with *echei*, "has," understood from the previous line.

12, 7–15 *So if you . . . at something else*: Here Plotinus addresses us, using the second person, and in the remainder of the chapter he describes the non-discursive experience of identity with the whole intelligible realm that is available to us.

The "search" that one no longer engages in at this stage (14) is typical for discursive reason (*dianoia*), which seeks because it does not yet possess the intended object of its thought (cf. IV.4.17, 1–7). Non-discursive thought possesses its object and therefore does not seek. On this see Emilsson (2007, ch. 4, sec. 1).

12, 15–24 *But if you . . . present to you*: The Aristotelian idea that in intellectual thought of things without matter the thinker is identical with its object is no doubt at work in 16–19. The subject, the thinker, as it were joins the universal Intellect, and makes its thoughts its own. Interestingly, Plotinus describes its thoughts as self-identifications in the first person (cf. V.3.10, 37ff.; V.3.13, 24; and Emilsson [2007, ch. 2, sec. 7], who, however, does not comment on this passage). The implication of Plotinus' words here is that the one who fully follows his recommendation will in the end say: "I am everything" where "everything" is understood as the whole intelligible realm.

The "addition" mentioned in 21 is no doubt the body and what comes with it. The identification of this with non-being in 22–23 only indicates a contrast with real intelligible being—in Platonic terms this would mean that the addition comes from becoming and not from being. It does not, of course, imply absolute non-existence.

There is a textual issue in 21–22. The translation here follows HS₂, which corrects *pantos* ("the whole") to *tou ontos* ("being"). This is partly based on a paraphrase in Porphyry's *Sententiae* 40, 2. The emendation is, however, strictly speaking not necessary, since the whole is clearly identical or at least coextensive with being in this treatise (cf. the inference from "not being" to "not whole" in 23 and 4.2, 13–14).

In 24 the notion of "abandoning the other things" (*apheis ta alla*) is brought in. As Tornau notes (*ad loc.*), this notion signifies the contrary of being occupied with the addition mentioned in 21 or, more precisely, the other things are exactly the addition to oneself that does not come from being. Ultimately, this is the non-being of matter that contaminates all corporeal existence. Plotinus employs similar phrases a number of times (cf., e.g., I.1.12, 23; V.3.4, 29; VI.8.21, 26).

12, 25–29 *But if it . . . is its opposite*: Plotinus develops the point that what is present to you depends on where you are turned. An ambiguity, no doubt intentional, in the phrase "being present," is, however, to be detected: in one sense the intelligible whole is present to us when and only when we turn toward it and it appears. In another sense (cf. 27–28), which turns out to be the favored sense, it is always present, irrespective of our apprehension of it. He even goes as far as holding that even when we, that is, our empirical selves (see Commentary 4.14, 16–17), have turned away from the intelligible, it is still present to us: it is just that we have, as it were, looked in the other direction. But to whom is it then present? The answer is no doubt to our own intelligible counterparts, which are there irrespective of the turnings of our empirical selves (cf. Commentary 4.14, 29–31).

12, 29–36 *For similarly other . . . his infinite unity*: The "other gods" in 29–32 are without doubt the gods of popular mythology and religion, as HBT suggests. The citation is from Homer, *Odyssey* 17, 486. Plato in *Republic* 2.381d1–4 censures these lines for presenting the gods as imposters. The reference to a god that only one person can see, however, fits the appearance of Athena in the *Iliad* 1, 194–200, where she appears only to Achilles. It is difficult to say whether Plotinus intends this literally, at least as a story that can be given an instructive allegorical interpretation, or whether he means to join Plato in questioning such stories.

Plotinus goes on to insist that there is a god to whom all cities, heaven and earth turn, a god who "remains by himself and in himself and possesses from himself being and the things that truly exist" (34–35). This god appears to be quite elevated. Is it the One itself or its first image, Intellect? The One has not been much explicitly present in our treatise (see, however, Commentary 5.4, 17–24; 5.5, 10–17; 5.9, 27–42). Still Plotinus might find it appropriate to refer to the first principle here at the end of the treatise. The god spoken of here has the air of an ultimate principle: everything depends on him and he possesses infinite unity (36), which does not so naturally fit the manifold Intellect. Despite this, much speaks in favor of Intellect, and this is what Tornau takes for granted: Intellect/being has been a theme in the discussion not only in the previous lines but throughout the treatise. This god is said to possess or hold (*echein*) "from himself being and the things that truly exist" (35): That the One, possesses (comprises, has) the true beings, is not Plotinus' normal way of describing the relation between the former and the latter, even if it arguably is true that the One in some sense has the true beings. So we conclude that Intellect is what Plotinus has in mind here. It is relevant, however, that, just as he is not so concerned in this treatise to distinguish between soul and Intellect, he is not so concerned either to distinguish between the Intellect and the One: the distinction he is concerned with is the one between sensible, spatial, items and non-sensible, intelligible, items.

Select Bibliography

I. Ancient Authors

Alexander Aphrodisiensis. 1887. *De anima*, edited by Ivo Bruns. Berlin: Reimer.

Aristotle. 1924 (repr. 1970 of 1953 corr. edn). *Metaphysica*, edited by W. D. Ross. Oxford: Clarendon Press.

———. 1964. *Analytica priora et posteriora*, edited by W. D. Ross. Oxford: Clarendon Press.

———. 1965. *Aristôte. Du ciel*, edited by Paul Moraux. Paris: Les Belles Lettres.

———. 1967. *De anima*, edited by W. D. Ross. Oxford: Clarendon Press.

Arnim, Hans von, ed. 1905. *Stoicorum Veterum Fragmenta*. Leipzig: Teubner.

Barnes, Jonathan, 1984. *The Complete Works of Aristotle, The Revised Oxford Translation*, edited by Jonathan Barnes, 2 vols. Princeton: Princeton University Press.

Cooper, John M. 1997. *Plato. Complete Works.* Edited, with Introduction and Notes, by John M. Cooper. Indianapolis: Hackett Publishing Company.

Diels, Hermann, and Walther Kranz. 1952. *Die Fragmente der Vorsokratiker*, vol. 2, 6th ed. Berlin: Weidmann.

Emilsson, Eyjólfur K. 1988. *Plotinus on Sense-Pereception: A Philosophical Study.* Cambridge: Cambridge University Press.

———. 2007. *Plotinus on Intellect.* Oxford: Oxford University Press.

Homer. 1931. *Ilias*, edited by Thomas W. Allen. Oxford: Clarendon Press.

———. 1962. *Odyssea*, edited by Peter von der Mühll. Basel: Helbing & Lichtenhahn.

Kirk, Geoffrey, Stephen Raven, and Malcolm Schofield. 1983. *The Presocratic Philosophers.* A Critical History with a Selection of Texts. Cambridge: Cambridge University Press.

Long, Anthony A., and David N. Sedley, trans. 1987. *The Hellenistic Philosophers*, vol. 1: *Translation of the Principal Sources, with Philosophical Commentary.* Cambridge: Cambridge University Press.

Marcus Aurelius. 1944. *The meditations of the emperor Marcus Aurelius*, vol. 1, edited by A. S. L. Farquharson. Oxford: Clarendon Press.

Nemesius. 1987. *Nemesii Emeseni De natura hominis*, edited by Moreno Morani. Leipzig: Teubner.

Numenius. 1974. *Numénius. Fragments*, edited by Édouard des Places. Paris: Les Belles Lettres.

Plato. 1900–1902. *Platonis opera*, vols. 1–4, edited by John Burnet. Oxford: Clarendon Press.

Plutarch. 1954. *Platonicae quaestiones*, edited by C. Hubert. Leipzig: Teubner.

Porphyry. 1975. *Sententiae ad intelligibilia ducentes*, edited by Erich Lamberz. Leipzig: Teubner.

———. 1964. "Vita Plotini." In *Plotini opera*, vol. 1, edited by Paul Henry, and Hans-Rudolf Schwyzer. Oxford: Clarendon Press.

Pythagoras. 1971. "Carmen aureum." In *Theognis*, edited by Douglas Young. Leipzig: Teubner.

Sallustius. 1960. *Des dieux et du monde*, edited by Gabriel Rochefort. Paris: Les Belles Lettres.

Simplicius. 1882. *In Aristotelis physicorum libros commentaria*, edited by Hermann Diels. Berlin: Reimer.

Stobaeus, Joannes. 1884–1912. *Anthologium*, edited by Curtius Wachsmuth, and Otto Hense, 5 vols. Berlin: Weidmann.

Xenocrates. 1892. *Darstellung der Lehre und Sammlung der Fragmente*, edited by Richard Heinze. Leipzig: Teubner.

II. Editions and Translations of the Enneads

Armstrong, Arthur Hilary. 1966–82. *Plotinus, Enneads*. Greek Text with English Translation and Introductions. Cambridge, MA: Loeb.

Bréhier, Émile. 1924–38. *Plotin, Ennéades*. Greek Text and French Translation with Introductions and Notes. Paris: Les Belles Lettres.

Cilento, Vincenzo. *Plotino, Enneadi*. Italian Translation and Commentary. Bari: Laterza.

Creuzer, Georg Friedrich. 1835. *Plotini Enneades*. Greek Text, with Marsilio Ficino's Latin Translation and Commentary. Oxford: E Typographeo Academico.

Harder, Richard, Robert Beutler, and Willy Theiler. 1956–71. *Plotins Schriften*. Greek Text with German Translation and Commentary. Hamburg: Meiner.

Henry, Paul and Hans-Rudolph Schwyzer. 1951–73. *Plotini Opera* I–III (editio maior). Paris: Desclée de Brouwer et Cie (HS₁).

———. 1964-82. *Plotini Opera* I–III (editio minor, with revised text). Oxford: Clarendon Press (HS₂).

Kirchhoff, Adolph, 1856. *Plotini Opera*. Leipzig: Teubner.

MacKenna, Stephen. 1991. *Plotinus. The Enneads*. Selected Treatises Revised with Notes by John Dillon. London: Penguin.

III. Studies on VI.4. and 5 and Related Works

Blumenthal, Henry J. 1971. *Plotinus' Psychology*. The Hague: Martinus Nijhoff.

Brisson, L. 1991. "Comment Plotin interprète-t-il les cinque genres du *Sophist*?" In *Études sur le Sophiste de Platon* (*Elenchos, Collana di testi e studi sul pensiero antico*, 21), edited by Pierre Aubenque and Michel Narcy, 449–473. Naples: Bibliopolis.

Chiaradonna, Riccardo. 2012. "Plotinus' Account of the Cognitive Powers of the Soul: Sense Perception and Discursive Thought." *Topoi* 31 (2), 191–207.

Cleary, John, ed. 1997. *The Perennial Tradition of Neoplatonism* (Ancient and Medieval Philosophy 1, 24). Leuven: Leuven University Press.

Corrigan, Kevin. 1996. "Essence and Existence in the *Enneads*." In *The Cambridge Companion to Plotinus*, edited by Lloyd P. Gerson, 105–129. Cambridge: Cambridge University Press.

D'Ancona Costa, Cristina. 1995. *Recherches sur le* Liber de causis (Études de Philosophie Médievale). Paris: J. Vrin.

Dodds, E. R. et al. 1960. *Les sources de Plotin* (Entretiens sur l'antiquité classique 5). Vandœuvres, Genève: Fondation Hardt.

Emilsson, Eyjólfur K. 1991. "Plotinus on Soul-Body Dualism." In *Psychology, Companions to Ancient Thought*, edited by Stephen Everson. Cambridge: Cambridge University Press.

————. 1994. "Plotinus' Ontology in *Ennead* VI.4 and 5." *Hermathena* 157, 87–101. In French, 1993 as "L'ontologie de Plotin dans l'Ennéade VI 4–5." In *Contre Platon 1: Le Platonisme dévoilé*, edited by *Monique* Dixsaut, 157–173. Paris: J. Vrin.

Gerson, Lloyd P. 1996. *The Cambridge Companion to Plotinus*, edited by Lloyd P. Gerson. Cambridge: Cambridge University Press.

————. 2012. "Plotinus on *logos*." In *Neoplatonism and the Philosophy of Nature,* edited by Christoph Horn and James Wilberding, 17–29. Oxford: Oxford University Press.

Henry, Paul. 1960 "Une comparaison chez Aristôte, Alexandre et Plotin." In *Les sources de Plotin* (Entretiens sur l'antiquité classique 5), 427–449. Vandœuvres, Genève: Fondation Hardt.

Igal, Jesus. 1975. "Sobre Plotini opera III de P. Henry y H.-R. Schwyzer." *Emerita* (43), 169–196.

————. 1979. "Aristoteles y la evolución de la antropología de Plotino." *Pensamiento Psicológico* 35, 315–345.

Kalligas, Paul 1997. "Forms of Individuals in Plotinus: A Re-Examination." *Phronesis* 42 (2), 206–227.

Kleist, Hugo von. 1881. *Der Gedankengang in Plotins erster Abhandlung über die Allgegenwart der intelligibeln in der wahrnehmbaren Welt* (Enn. VI, 4). K. Gymnasium und Realschule I. Ordnung zu Flensburg, Jahresbericht.

Lee, J. Scott. 1979. "The Doctrine of Reception according to the Capacity of the Recipient in *Ennead* VI.4–5. *Dionysius Halifax* 3, 79–97.

Leibniz, Gottlieb Friedrich, Freiherr von. 1840. Letter to Hansch, July 16, 1716. In *Opera philosophica quae exstant latina, gallica, germanica omnia* I, edited by Joannes Eduadrus Erdmann, 455. Berlin: G. Eichleri.

Lloyd, Anthony C. 1986. "Plotinus on the Genesis of Thought and Existence." *Oxford Studies in Ancient Philosophy* 5, 155–186.

———. 1989. *The Anatomy of Neoplatonism*. Oxford: Oxford University Press.

Magrin, Sarah. 2010. "Sensation and Scepticism in Plotinus." *Oxford Studies in Ancient Philosophy* 39, 249–297.

Morelli, Eric J. 2011. "Plotinus' Two Interpretations of *Timaeus* 35a." *Ancient Philosophy* 31, 351–361.

Noble, Christopher. 2013. "How Plotinus' Soul Animates his Body: The Argument for the Soul-Trace at *Ennead* IV.4.18.1–9." *Phronesis* 58 (3), 249–279.

O'Brien, Denis. 1991. *Plotinus on the Origin of Matter.* Naples: Bibliopolis.

———. 1996. "Plotinus on Matter and Evil." In the Cambridge Companion to Plotinus, edited by Lloyd P. Gerson, 171–195. Cambridge: Cambridge University Press.

O'Daly, Gerard, J. P. 1973. *Plotinus' Philosophy of the Self.* Shannon: Irish University Press.

O'Meara, Dominic J. 1980. "The Problem of Omnipresence in Plotinus, *Ennead* VI, 4–5: A Reply." *Dionysius* 4, 61–73. Halifax: Dalhousie University Department of Classics.

Pépin, Jean. 1971. "Héraclès et son reflet dans le Néoplatonisme." In *Le Néoplatonisme* (Colloques internationaux du Centre National de la Recherche Scientifique [Royaumont, June 9–13, 1969]), 167–192. Paris: CNRS.

Remes, Pauliina. 2007. "*Plotinus on Self: The Philosophy of the 'We'.*" Cambridge: Cambridge University Press.

Santa Cruz de Prunes, Maria Isabel. 1997. "L'exégèse plotinienne des μέγιστα γένη du *Sophiste* de Platon. In *The Perennial Tradition of Neoplatonism*, edited by John Cleary, 105–118. Leuven: Leuven University Press

Schroeder, Frederic M. 1992. *Form and Transformation: A Study in the Philosophy of Plotinus*. Montreal: McGill-Queen's University Press.

Schwyzer, Hans-Rudolph. 1935. "Zu Plotins Interpretation von Platons *Timaeus* 35 A." In *Rheinisches Museum für Philologie* 84 (4), 360–368.

Smith, Andrew. 1974. *Porphyry's Place in the Neoplatonic Tradition: A Study in Post-Plotinian Neoplatonism*. The Hague: Martinus Nijhoff.

———. 1996. "Plotinus on the Nature of Eternity and Time." In *The Cambridge Companion to Plotinus*, edited by Lloyd M. Gerson, 196–216. Cambridge: Cambridge University Press.

———. 2006. "The object of perception in Plotinus." In *Eriugena, Berkeley, and the idealist tradition*, edited by Stephen Gersh and Dermot Moran, 95–104. Notre Dame, IN: University of Notre Dame Press.

Strange, Steven K. 1992. "Plotinus' Account of Participation In *Ennead* VI.4–5." *Journal of The History of Philosophy* 30 (4), 479–496.

———. 1994. "Plotinus on the Nature of Eternity and Time." In *Aristotle in Late Antiquity* (Studies in Philosophy and the History of Philosophy 27), edited by Lawrence P. Schrenk, 22–53. Washington D.C.: The Catholic University of America Press.

Taylor, Richard C. 1998. "Aquinas, the *Plotiniana Arabica*, and the Metaphysics of Being and Actuality," *Journal of the History of Ideas* 59 (2), 217–239.

Tomarchio, John. 1999. "Thomistic Axiomatics in an Age of Computers." In *History of Philosophy Quarterly* 16 (3), 163–187.

Tornau, Christian. 1998. *Plotin. Enneaden VI 4–5 [22–23]. Ein Kommentar*. Stuttgart and Leipzig: B. G. Teubner.

———. 1998. "Wissenschaft, Seele, Geist: Zur Bedeutung einer Analogie bei Plotin (*Enn.* IV 9,5 und VI 2,20)," *Göttinger Forum für Altertumswissenschaft* 1, 87–111.

Wilberding, James. 2006. *Plotinus' Cosmology: A Study of* Ennead *II. 1 (40): Text, Translation, and Commentary*. Oxford: Oxford University Press.

IV. General Publications

Alt, K. 1993. *Weltflucht und Weltbejahung. Zur Frage des Leib-Seele Dualismus bei Plutarch, Numenius, Plotin*. Stuttgart: Franz Steiner Verlag.

Armstrong, A. H. 1940. *The Architecture of the Intelligible Universe in the Philosophy of Plotinus*. Cambridge: Cambridge University Press.

⸻: (ed.). 1967. *The Cambridge History of Later Greek and Early Mediaeval Philosophy.* Cambridge: Cambridge University Press.

Arnou, R. 1968. *Le Désir de Dieu dans la philosophie de Plotin.* 2nd ed. Rome: Presses de l'Université Grégorienne.

Dillon, J. 1977/1996. *The Middle Platonists: A Study of Platonism, 80 B.C.–A.D. 220,* London: Duckworth, 1977, 1996².

Emilsson, E. K. 1988. *Plotinus on Sense-Perception.* Cambridge: Cambridge University Press.

⸻: 2007. *Plotinus on Intellect.* Oxford: The Clarendon Press.

Gatti, M. L. 1996. *Plotino e la metafisica della contemplazione,* Milan: Vita e Pensiero.

Gerson, L. P. 1994. *Plotinus,* London/New York: Routledge.

⸻: (ed.). 1996. *The Cambridge Companion to Plotinus,* Cambridge: Cambridge University Press.

⸻: (ed.). 2010. *The Cambridge History of Philosophy in Late Antiquity.* 2 vols. Cambridge: Cambridge University Press.

Gottschalk, H. B. 1980. *Heraclides of Pontus,* Oxford: Oxford University Press.

Guthrie, W. K. C. 1967–1978. *A History of Greek Philosophy,* 5 vols., Cambridge: Cambridge University Press.

Hadot, Pierre. 1993. *Plotinus on the Simplicity of Vision.* Translated by M. Chase. Chicago: Chicago University Press.

Inge, W. R. 1948. *The Philosophy of Plotinus.* 3rd ed. London: Longmans, Green.

Les Sources de Plotin, 1960. Entretiens Fondation Hardt V. Vandoeuvres-Genève.

Lloyd, Anthony C. 1990. *The Anatomy of Neoplatonism.* Oxford: Clarendon Press.

Meijer, P. A. 1992. Plotinus *on the Good or the One (Enneads VI, 9): An Analytical Commentary*, Amsterdam: J. C. Gieben.

O'Daly, G. 1973. *Plotinus' Philosophy of the Self*, Irish University Press: Shannon.

O'Meara, Dominic J., 1993. *Plotinus: an Introduction to the Enneads.* Oxford: Oxford University Press.

Pépin, J. 1958. *Mythe et allégorie: les origins grecques et les contestations judéo-chrétiennes.* Paris: Aubier.

Remes, Pauliina. 2008. *Neoplatonism.* Berkeley: University of California Press.

Rist, John M., 1967. *Plotinus: The Road to Reality.* Cambridge: Cambridge University Press.

Schniewind, Alexandrine. 2003. *L'Éthique du Sage chez Plotin.* Paris: J. Vrin.

Smith, A. 1974. *Porphyry's Place in the Neoplatonic Tradition: A Study in Post-Plotinian Neoplatonism*, The Hague: Nijhoff.

———: 1981. "Potentiality and the Problem of Plurality in the Intelligible," in *Neoplatonism and Early Christian Thought*, edd. H. J. Blumenthal and R. A. Markus. London: Variorum, 99–107.

———: 2004. *Philosophy in Late Antiquity*. London: Routledge.

Theiler, W. 1960. "Plotin zwischen Platon und Stoa," in *Les Sources de Plotin*, Entretiens Fondation Hardt V, Vandoeuvres-Genève: Fondation Hardt, 63–103.

Wallis, R. T. 1995. *Neoplatonism*. 2nd ed. London: Duckworth.

West, M. L. 1966. *Hesiod* Theogony, *Edited with Prolegomena and Commentary*. Oxford: Clarendon Press.

Index of Ancient Authors

Index of Names and Subjects

PRE-SOCRATICS

By Being, It Is: The Thesis of Parmenides by Néstor-Luis Cordero

Parmenides and the History of Dialectic: Three Essays by Scott Austin

Parmenides, Venerable and Awesome: Proceedings of the International Symposium edited by Néstor-Luis Cordero

The Fragments of Parmenides: A Critical Text with Introduction and Translation, the Ancient Testimonia and a Commentary by A. H. Coxon. Revised and Expanded Edition edited with new Translations by Richard McKirahan and a new Preface by Malcolm Schofield

The Legacy of Parmenides: Eleatic Monism and Later Presocratic Thought by Patricia Curd

The Route of Parmenides: Revised and Expanded Edition, With a New Introduction, Three Supplemental Essays, and an Essay by Gregory Vlastos by Alexander P. D. Mourelatos

To Think Like God: Pythagoras and Parmenides. The Origins of Philosophy. Scholarly and fully annotated edition by Arnold Hermann

The Illustrated To Think Like God: Pythagoras and Parmenides. The Origins of Philosophy by Arnold Hermann with over 200 full color illustrations

Presocratics and Plato: A Festschrift in Honor of Charles Kahn edited by Richard Patterson, Vassilis Karasmanis, and Arnold Hermann

PLATO

A Stranger's Knowledge: Statesmanship, Philosophy, and Law in Plato's Statesman by Xavier Márquez

God and Forms in Plato by Richard D. Mohr

Image and Paradigm in Plato's Sophist by David Ambuel

Interpreting Plato's Dialogues by J. Angelo Corlett

One Book, the Whole Universe: Plato's Timaeus *Today* edited by Richard D. Mohr and Barbara M. Sattler

Platonic Patterns: *A Collection of Studies* by Holger Thesleff

Plato's Late Ontology: *A Riddle Resolved* by Kenneth M. Sayre

Plato's Parmenides: *Text, Translation & Introductory Essay* by Arnold Hermann. Translation in collaboration with Sylvana Chrysakopoulou with a Foreword by Douglas Hedley

Plato's Universe by Gregory Vlastos

The Philosopher in Plato's Statesman by Mitchell Miller

ARISTOTLE

Aristotle's Empiricism: Experience and Mechanics in the Fourth Century B.C. by Jean De Groot

One and Many in Aristotle's Metaphysics—*Volume I: Books Alpha-Delta* by Edward C. Halper

One and Many in Aristotle's Metaphysics—*Volume 2: The Central Books* by Edward C. Halper

Reading Aristotle: Physics VII.3 "What is Alteration?" *Proceedings of the International ESAP-HYELE Conference* edited by Stefano Maso, Carlo Natali, and Gerhard Seel

HELLENISTIC PHILOSOPHY

A Life Worthy of the Gods: *The Materialist Psychology of Epicurus* by David Konstan

THE *ENNEADS* OF PLOTINUS

Translations with Introductions & Philosophical Commentaries

Series edited by John M. Dillon and Andrew Smith

Enneads VI.4 & VI.5: On the Presence of Being, One and the Same, Everywhere as a Whole by Eyjólfur Emilsson and Steven Strange

Ennead IV.8: On the Descent of the Soul into Bodies by Barrie Fleet

Ennead V.5: That the Intelligibles are not External to the Intellect, and on the Good by Lloyd P. Gerson

ETHICS

Sentience and Sensibility: *A Conversation about Moral Philosophy* by Matthew R. Silliman

PHILOSOPHICAL FICTION

Pythagorean Crimes by Tefcros Michaelides

The Aristotle Quest: A Dana McCarter Trilogy. Book 1: Black Market Truth by Sharon M. Kaye

AUDIOBOOKS
The Iliad (unabridged) by Stanley Lombardo
The Odyssey (unabridged) by Stanley Lombardo
The Essential Homer by Stanley Lombardo
The Essential Iliad by Stanley Lombardo

FORTHCOMING
Plato in the Empire: Albinus, Maximus, Apuleius. *Text, Translation, and Commentary* by Ryan C. Fowler

FORTHCOMING TITLES IN THE SERIES
THE *ENNEADS* OF PLOTINUS
Translations with Introductions & Philosophical Commentaries
Series edited by John M. Dillon and Andrew Smith

Ennead I.2: On Virtues by Suzanne Stern-Gillet
Ennead I.6: On Beauty by Andrew Smith
Ennead II.4: On Matter by Anthony A. Long
Ennead II.5: On What Exists Potentially and What Actually by Cinzia Arruzza
Ennead II.9: Against the Agnostics by Sebastian Ramon Philipp Gertz
Ennead III.8: On Nature and Contemplation by George Karamanolis
Ennead IV.3–4.29: Problems concerning the Soul by John M. Dillon and H. J. Blumenthal
Ennead IV.1–2, IV.4.30–45 & IV.5: Problems concerning the Soul by Gary M. Gurtler
Ennead IV.7: On the Immortality of the Soul by Barrie Fleet
Ennead V.1: On the Three Principial Hypostases by Eric D. Perl
Ennead V.8: On Intelligible Beauty by Andrew Smith
Ennead VI.8: On Free Will and the Will of the One by Kevin Corrigan and John D. Turner